MY NEIGHBOUR'S FAITH

MY NEIGHBOUR'S FAITH

Islam Explained for African Christians

JOHN AZUMAH

My Neighbour's Faith
Copyright © 2008 by John Azumah

Published 2008 by **Hippo** Books

This edition published for

WordAlive Publishers, PO Box 4547 GPO-00100 Nairobi, Kenya
www.wordalivepublishers.org

Africa Christian Textbooks (ACTS), TCNN, PMB 2020, Bukuru 930008,
Plateau State, Nigeria
www.africachristiantextbooks.com

Zondervan, Grand Rapids, Michigan 49530
www.zondervan.com

ISBN 978 9966 805 02 7

All quotations from the Qur'ān are from the translation by M. Pickthall, as contained
in the Alim CD-ROM (Baltimore, MD: ISL Software Corporation, 1986–2000).
References to the Qur'ān are identified by sura (chapter) and verse. A reference to
33:21 therefore stands for Qur'ān chapter 33, verse 21.

All quotations from the Bible are taken from the Revised Standard Version, as
contained in BibleWorks, CD-ROM version 4.0.035p (Norfolk, VA: BibleWorks,
1998). Copyright © 1946, 1952, 1971 by the Division of Christian Education of
the National Council of Churches of Christ in the USA. Used by permission.

Cover design: WordAlive Publishers

Book design To a Tee Ltd, www.2at.com

To the Rev. Canon Dr. David & Robyn Claydon

In appreciation for their pastoral care, support and wise counsel to our family during and after our time in India as missionaries with CMS-Australia. Dr. Claydon is the immediate past General Secretary of CMS-Australia and the International Director of the Lausanne Committee for World Evangelization. Dr. Claydon's pastoral care and deep practical insights into mission issues have been a source of great inspiration to me.

Contents

Foreword

The start of the twenty-first century has been marked by two major developments relating to religion in the world. First, Christianity has become a predominantly non-Western religion, with its heartlands firmly located in the southern continents of Africa, Asia and South America. The assumption that Christianity is the religion of the West, an assumption that has persisted for nearly a thousand years, is being succeeded by a growing realisation that the West has become post-Christian.

Second, in the wake of the armed attack on the United States of America by radical Muslims on September 11, 2001, Islam has attracted widespread media attention across the world and is now perceived as representing the public face of religious commitment. For many who are unaware of the new Christian configuration of the world today, the September 11 attack was tantamount to an Islamic assault on the 'Christian West'. One effect of the attack and its aftermath in the Middle East and elsewhere has been a deepening and entrenching of the perception of irreconcilable differences between the two main missionary religions in the world.

At the same time, post-modernist and post-colonial Western discourse tends to practice voluntary censorship in its approach to Islam. Although the treatment of Christian history, teaching and tradition is often critical and even hostile, the treatment of Islamic history, teaching and tradition is quite different, perhaps because several Islamic nations are considered vital to the economic interests of the West.

All this means that, at the level of religion, Christian–Muslim relations have become quite prone to distortion when viewed primarily through the Western experience. In most of the West, Muslims and persons of religions other than Christianity have for many years been perceived as "the irreducible other". The absence of regular experience of religious pluralism also means that Western Christian affirmations have been made with little reference to the faiths of others. This Western handicap is compounded by the now prevailing view that deeply held religious convictions are harmful to the interests and concerns of modern society.

Circumstances in Africa are very different, which makes John Azumah's approach to Islam important and refreshing. He writes from the perspective of someone raised in a Ghanaian multifaith family. His Muslim uncle made significant contributions towards his theological training, and some 95 per cent of the family members who attended his ordination as a Presbyterian minister were Muslim. This uniquely African interreligious and interfaith environment means that he does not approach Islam as an impersonal system of beliefs or as the religion of immigrant communities, but as a religion with "a human face: the face of a close relative, a neighbour." Dr Azumah's aim is to help African Christians understand their neighbours' faith.

Dr Azumah neither demonises nor romanticises Islam. He writes as a Christian teacher and pastor, with concern for Muslims as persons who should be treated with respect and love. This respect and love does not preclude inviting them to consider the truth claims of the good news about Jesus.

Dr Azumah demonstrates that Christian mission need not be regarded as incompatible with dialogue between different faiths. On the contrary, the missionary character of both Islam and Christianity precludes such incompatibility. On a continent where the two faiths meet, probably for the first time, on something approaching an equal footing, *My Neighbour's Faith* represents a valuable contribution to the mission of Christian scholarship.

Kwame Bediako
Akropong-Akuapem, Ghana
Pentecost 2007

Acknowledgements

I wish to express my sincere gratitude to the following individuals who have offered support, suggestions and criticisms as I have worked on this book.

Pearl Amanor, Senior Publications Assistant of the Akrofi-Christaller Institute, was the first to read through the draft of the manuscript. Her useful suggestions on style and expressions made me take time to 'listen to myself' as I developed the issues further.

Hazel Squires, a very good friend and colleague, read through the final draft. Her corrections and extremely helpful comments enabled me to develop the content and flow of the material.

Every writer needs as professional and understanding an editor as Isobel Stevenson. She is a thorough professional, who followed up references, checked page numbers and quotations, and cross-checked key aspects of the content. Isobel's eagle editorial eye saved me from what could have been embarrassing slips. Her many questions were always couched in friendly and uplifting terms.

By divine design, Angela Addy, Deputy Publications Officer of the Akrofi-Christaller Institute, was able to work on this manuscript while on a training course with Isobel in Canada. Angela, who knew me personally, made very useful contributions to the editing of the manuscript.

To all of you, I say a big THANK YOU. May God richly bless you!

I have to state, however, that I take full responsibility for the ideas expressed in this book and am solely responsible for any of its shortcomings.

1

Introduction

Africa has an interreligious and interfaith environment that is unique in many ways. We have multifaith families, clans, ethnic groups and nations. At each of these levels, African Muslims and Christians have a lot of things that bind them together, including kinship ties, shared languages and citizenship. If I may use my own case as an example, I come from a family where believers in Traditional African Religion, Muslims and Christians live and share basically everything. My Muslim uncle made significant contributions towards my theological training and about 95 per cent of the family members who attended my ordination service were Muslim. Similarly, when there is anything involving a family member, all members of the family, irrespective of their religious affiliation, are called upon to contribute.

At the national level, Ghana has a Catholic president, and a Muslim vice-president who were sworn into office by a lay Methodist chief justice. Similar examples of pluralist realities are fairly common across sub-Saharan Africa.

The other side of the coin is that most of the inhuman acts perpetrated by human beings have, directly or indirectly, something to do with religion. As one theologian writing on religion and violence observes:

> Many of the violent conflicts in the world today involve religious animosities. Indeed, the history of the encounters among the world's religions is filled with distrust and hatred, violence and vengeance. The deepest tragedy of the history of religions is that the very movements that should bring human beings closer to each other and to their ultimate source and goal have time and time again become forces of division. In one conflict after another around the world, religious convictions

and interpretations of revelation have been used and abused as justifications for violence.[1]

Again speaking from my own context, in 1995 Ghana had her fair share of interreligious confrontations, mainly between Christians and Muslims in Takoradi, Kumasi and Tamale. The conflicts involving Christians and Muslims in places like Sudan, Nigeria and Ivory Coast are well known. These conflicts have their roots in the collective historical experience of Africans as well as in present socio-political and religious challenges. Some would argue, however, that ignorance accounts for much of the fear, suspicion and hatred that lead to violence and open conflicts between people of different religions. On both the Christian and Muslim sides in Africa, there is a lot of ignorance, prejudice and stereotyping. How do we maintain peace between the Christian and Muslim communities?

In the words of Mother Theresa, 'peace is not something you wish for, it's something you make, something you do, something you are, something you give away.' Also talking about religion and peace, the prominent Swiss theologian Hans Küng made the following solemn observation:

> No world peace without peace among religions; no peace among religions without dialogue between the religions; and no dialogue between the religions without accurate knowledge of one another.[2]

There is therefore an urgent need for accurate knowledge of the teaching and beliefs of religions other than our own. The British Prime Minister Tony Blair is right when he says, 'Knowledge dispels fear. Knowledge clears away misunderstanding. Knowledge strengthens trust.'[3]

Over the last half century, there have been many discussions and activities aimed at promoting better understanding between people of different religious traditions and civilisations. One of the positive results of these endeavours is the proliferation of study centres and literature in the West aimed at presenting Islam in a more sympathetic and positive light.

---

[1] Leo D. Lefebure, *Revelations, the Religions, and Violence* (New York: Orbis Books, 2000): 7–8.
[2] H. Küng, 'Christianity and world religions: Dialogue with Islam', in L. Swidler (ed.), *Toward a Universal Theology of Religion* (Maryknoll NY: Orbis Books, 1987): 194.
[3] The text of Blair's speech to Christian and Muslim academics is included in Michael Ipgrave (ed.), *The Road Ahead: A Christian–Muslim Dialogue* (London: Church House Publishing, 2002): xiv.

This is a welcome departure from the medieval demonisation of Islam and nineteenth-century Western polemics against it. In the wake of 11 September 2001, the need to carry on with this task has become even more urgent. Many Western journalists, politicians, clergy and academics have taken up this task and are genuinely trying to help redress the situation. This is certainly a valid and welcome undertaking in our increasingly pluralistic and interdependent world.

The problem, however, is that the drive to address past misconceptions has brought about another unhealthy tendency, referred to by Bernard Lewis as 'voluntary censorship'.[4] Western scholars in particular, have tended to take a very critical and sometimes hostile view of the Christian tradition and heritage. However, they do not apply the same critical approach when dealing with Islamic teaching and history. As a direct result, mainline post-colonial Western discourse on Islam has, in the view of many, moved from extreme Islamophobia (the fear and demonisation of Islam) to what some have termed Islamophilia (the love and romanticisation of Islam).

Another reason for self-censorship is identified by Thomas L. Friedman in his response to the protests and sporadic violence that flared up across the Muslim world in response to Pope Benedict XVI's critical comments about Islam in September 2006:

> The pope was actually treating Islam with dignity. He was treating the faith and its community as adults who could be challenged and engaged. That is a sign of respect. What is insulting is the politically correct, kid-gloves views of how to deal with Muslims that is taking root in the West today. It goes like this:
>
> 'Hushhh! Don't say anything about Islam! Don't you understand? If you say anything critical or questioning about Muslims, they'll burn down your house. Hushhh! Just let them be. Don't rile them. They are not capable of a civil, rational dialogue about problems in their faith community.'
>
> Now that is insulting. It's an attitude full of contempt and self-censorship, but that is the attitude of Western elites today, and it's helping to foster the slow-motion clash of civilizations that Sam Huntington predicted. Because Western masses don't

---

[4] B. Lewis, *Islam and the West* (New York: Oxford University Press, 1993): 130.

buy it. They see violence exploding from Muslim communities and they find it frightening, and they don't think their leaders are talking honestly about it. So many now just want to build a wall against Islam.[5]

In the wake of the 11 September 2001 terrorist attack on America, interest in Islam amongst Christians across the world has been on the increase. We read about and see Muslims blowing themselves and others up in the name of their religion, while at the same time we hear Muslim leaders and Western experts proclaiming that Islam is a religion of peace. One theological student in India once said to me, 'Sir, I am confused! We hear Islam is a religion of peace, but we also read about and see Muslims praying with AK-47 rifles and teenage girls shot dead or disfigured for not wearing a veil!' He is not alone in his confusion. Thomas Friedman, who has lived in the Muslim world, enjoyed the friendship of many Muslims and seen the compassionate side of Islam, writes:

> On the first day of Ramadan last year a Sunni Muslim suicide bomber blew up a Shiite mosque in Hilla, Iraq, in the middle of a memorial service, killing 25 worshippers. This year on the first day of Ramadan, a Sunni suicide bomber in Baghdad killed 35 people who were lining up in a Shiite neighbourhood to buy fuel. The same day, the severed heads of nine murdered Iraqi police officers and soldiers were found north of Baghdad. I don't get it. How can Muslims blow up other Muslims on their most holy day of the year – in mosques! – and there is barely a peep of protest in the Muslim world, let alone a million Muslim march? Yet Danish cartoons or a papal speech lead to violent protests.[6]

Of course there are problems within all faith communities. But that is not the point. The point is that believers should be prepared to confront and deal with issues honestly in a mature and level-headed manner.

To add to the confusion, Islam itself is far from being a monolithic entity. There are Muslims who assert and genuinely believe that Islam is a religion of peace, while there are others whose discourse and activities

---

[5] Thomas L. Friedman, 'Islam and the Pope', in *International Herald Tribune*, September 30–October 1, 2006: 7.
[6] Ibid.

proclaim the opposite. Both claim that their version of Islam is the 'true' Islam. It has to be said that what does or does not constitute true Islam is a legitimate internal Muslim discussion that Christians can only join as detached commentators. In my view, Christians should concern themselves with matters in Islam that directly relate to them. In other words, Islam has a lot to say to and about Christians and Christianity in its scripture, traditions and theology, and Christians need to know these things. As one leading Muslim scholar put it:

> Islam's attitude to Christianity is as old as Islam itself, since Islam partly took shape by adopting certain important ideas from Judaism and Christianity and criticizing others. Indeed, Islam's self-definition is partly the result of its attitude to these two and their communities.[7]

In other words, right from the beginning, Islam has always defined itself in contradistinction to the other religions, especially Judaism and Christianity.

What I shall attempt to do in this book is to throw some light on the beliefs and teaching of Islam for Christians. In doing this, I shall touch on some matters that I consider of contemporary importance to Christians and the wider non-Muslim audience. I shall draw heavily from mainline Muslim sources and shall strive to avoid the two extremes of demonising and romanticising Islam. I shall always endeavour to keep the human face of Islam in mind. In Africa, as already noted, Islam is not an impersonal system of beliefs or the religion of immigrant communities. Rather, Islam has a human face: the face of a close relative, a neighbour, a teacher and even a head of state.

At the same time I have my academic integrity to protect. Hence, I will try to present the facts, including the hard facts, in the conviction that good relations can only be built on accurate and critical knowledge of self and one another. In addition I believe it is vital to provide Christian theological students with credible and balanced information in order to prevent them from being misinformed by other unhelpful material on the market or simply wall themselves off.

---

[7] Fazlur Rahman, *Major Themes of the Qurʾān* (Minneapolis: Bibliotheca Islamica, 1980): 162.

2

The Challenges Posed by Islam

To appreciate why it is important for Christians to study Islam, we need to know some of the key challenges Islam poses to Christian thought and theology in Africa. In this chapter, I will highlight some of these challenges.[1]

Existential Challenge

Other faiths, and especially Islam, are no longer known to us merely as concepts and labels but have acquired the faces of real people, whose presence affects many aspects of our Christian life. Thus in the West, which for a long time thought of itself as 'Christian', there are now religious minorities who are not foreigners but fully-fledged citizens. And although religious plurality has been part of African societies for centuries, it was only after independence that Africans realised the serious implications of the artificial political boundaries drawn by colonialists. People of different religions now have to relate to each other in ways they did not in pre-colonial and colonial times. In Ghana, for instance, Christians make up nearly 69 per cent of the population and Muslims about 16 per cent.[2] The president is a practising Catholic, and an equally practising Muslim is the vice-president. There is hardly any town or village in Ghana today where one cannot find Muslims and Christians living side by side, either as minorities or majorities.

These new realities have come with new challenges. Our socio-political, economic and educational structures and systems are affected,

---

[1] For further discussion of these challenges, see John Azumah 'Issues in Christian–Muslim relations: Implications for theological formation in Africa', in *Journal of African Christian Thought*, Vol. 7 No. 2, Dec. 2004: 3038.
[2] Figures taken from the 2000 Population and Housing Census released by the Statistical Service of Ghana.

and so is the way we think about and interact with people who belong to other religions. In many countries across the world, these challenges have erupted into violence and wars.

The church has recognised the reality of the challenge that religious diversity poses to societies. A document produced by the Second Vatican Council of the Roman Catholic Church in 1964 sums up the importance of understanding people of other faiths:

> In this age of ours, when men are drawing more closely together and the bonds of friendship between different peoples are being strengthened, the Church examines with greater care the relation which she has to non-Christian religions.[3]

Similarly, at a meeting in Nairobi in 1971, the Central Committee of the World Council of Churches (WCC) declared that dialogue with people of other religions is inevitable and urgent

> because everywhere in the world Christians are now living in pluralistic societies. It is urgent because all men are under common pressures in the search for justice, peace and a hopeful future.[4]

In places like Ghana, Muslims and Christians have often lived as close relations and neighbours. At the grass-roots level, they have on the whole lived in peace. Muslim relatives and friends visit Christians at Christmas to wish them well, and Christians in turn visit their Muslim friends and relatives during Islamic festivals. On these occasions, gifts and meals are shared. At weddings and child-naming ceremonies, and even at the ordination of priests, Muslims are known to come to church, and Christians attend Muslim gatherings when a ceremony involves a friend or relative. But Christians need to think about the questions such co-existence raises for Christian theology and mission.

---

[3] Austin Flannery (ed.), *Vatican II: The Conciliar and Post-Conciliar Documents* (Bombay: St Pauls Publications, 1975): 667.
[4] S. J. Samartha (ed.), *Living Faiths and the Ecumenical Movement* (Geneva: World Council of Churches, 1971): 47.

Intellectual Challenge

In Africa, the post-colonial elite opinion is that the African human, material and cultural heritage has been undermined by encounters with the Christian West through the trans-Atlantic slave trade, missionary activities and colonialism. Some have called for an outright rejection of Christianity; the majority agree on the continuing need to adapt it to suit African culture and the African historical and contemporary experience. Scores of works aimed at addressing (and redressing) the mishaps and mischief of this historical encounter have been produced. This critical attitude towards the Christian tradition in Africa is also a permanent feature of post-colonial African Christian thought. The dominant trend has been to de-Westernise the Christian tradition and to Africanise it as much as possible.

The Arab-Islamic dispensation appears to have been subjected to an entirely different analysis, resulting in a very different perception of post-colonial Africa's encounter with Arab-Islam. It is claimed that Islam, unlike Christianity, is an African religion, or that it is more in tune with the African personality and heritage than its Western-Christian rival. The group known as the Nation of Islam in America and Britain appeal to Africans in the Diaspora to convert, or rather revert, to Islam, which they claim is the original religion of Africa. They portray Christianity as the religion of the former slave-masters from whom Africans must sever all ties. These claims imply that African traditional values fared better in encounters with the Arab-Islamic tradition than in encounters with Christianity.

Most African Muslim scholars have taken these claims to their logical conclusion. They insist that the socio-political and economic woes of Africa are a direct result of the Western-Christian legacy, and that the solution lies in the adoption (if not enforcement) of an Arab-Islamic dispensation. At an Islamic conference in 1989 in Abuja, Nigeria, scores of African Muslim scholars and activists decried Western cultural and ideological influences in Africa. They lamented the continent's predicament as 'the object of [Western] imperial plunder' and 'a dumping ground for [Western] cultural and ideological ideas'. They resolved to 'encourage the teaching of Arabic ... as the lingua franca of the continent' and to 'struggle to re-instate the application of the

Shari'a'.[5] In other words, after diagnosing the cause of Africa's woes as Christian imperialism, the participants prescribed Arab-Islamic cultural, linguistic and religious imperialism as the solution.

The Abuja conference led to the founding of the Islam in Africa Organisation. The preamble to its charter speaks of its members being

> desirous of forging a common front to unite the Ummah with the view of facing the common enemies – the imperialist and Zionist forces of domination and secularisation, illiteracy, poverty and degradation – and to rediscover and reinstate *Africa's glorious Islamic past* (my emphasis).[6]

Radical Muslim activists are even more explicit in proposing Arab-Islam as the solution to Africa's problems. Referring to the chief ideologue of the nineteenth-century northern Nigerian jihad movement, the influential Nigerian Muslim scholar and activist Shehu Umar Abdullahi declared:

> The ideas of Shaikh Abdullahi dan-Fodio, when translated into some Nigerian languages, can be instrumental in solving [Nigeria's] chronic political instability, economic aridity, social perturbance and juridical nonsense.[7]

The main problem with such romantic conclusions is that they are based on a highly selective, revisionist history. Historical facts like the Muslim involvement in slavery and the savagery of the Muslim jihad in the eighteenth and nineteenth centuries are either glossed over or simply denied. The leaders of that jihad, who were the Bin Ladens of their time, are glorified and hailed as heroes and inspiring role models. Sanitised versions of their activities are taught as history in the schools across Africa, without any mention of the mass murder and enslavement the

---

[5] N. Alkali et al. (eds.), *Islam in Africa: Proceedings of the Islam in Africa Conference* (Ibadan: Spectrum, 1993): 432–33.

[6] J. Hunwick, 'Sub-Saharan Africa and the wider world of Islam: Historical and contemporary perspectives', in E. E. Rosander and D. Westerlund (eds.), *African Islam and Islam in Africa: Encounters between Sufis and Islamists* (London: Hurst, 1997): 41.

[7] Shehu Umar Abdullahi, *On the Search for a Viable Political Culture: Reflections on the Political Thought of Shaikh 'Abdullâhi Dan-Fodio* (Kaduna: Commercial Printing Dept, 1984): 5. The title of the book speaks for itself. For more discussion of such claims, see John Azumah, *The Legacy of Arab-Islam in Africa: A Quest for Inter-Religious Dialogue* (Oxford: Oneworld Publications, 2001), especially chapters 1 and 3.

jihad engendered. A cousin of mine, a university graduate, admitted he had never heard any mention of Muslim slavery in and outside Africa.

Such revisionist history has resulted, firstly, in the creation of a glamorous Islamic past, which feeds into the propaganda machine of Islamic fundamentalism. Radical Muslims look back to this mythical golden age of Islam and aspire to re-establish it. Secondly, the revisionist history has distorted local histories, with serious implications for Christian–Muslim relations. What is presented as history in books is not the history that the people on the ground remember from their oral histories and their own experience. Thirdly, Christians in the West have allowed this one-sided and hostile approach to the Christian past to create a sense of inherited guilt and loss of confidence in the gospel. This attitude has become a stumbling block to missions. Amazingly, many leading African Christian scholars quote this sanitised, one-sided, revisionist history and blatant propaganda as fact. Thus an All Africa Conference of Churches (AACC) report on its 1969 Assembly in Abidjan observed that 'Islam is held [in Africa] to be an African religion, with almost no foreign missionaries, which tolerates African traditions.'[8] This unsupported statement is used to challenge the African church to take the inculturation of Christianity in Africa seriously. Unless the sanitised and revisionist versions of the history of Islam in Africa is challenged, African Christians risk the same loss of confidence and inherited guilt complex as their Western co-religionists.

Territorial/Demographic Challenge

Islam, more than any other religion, has demographically displaced Christianity from what used to be Christian heartlands in the Middle East, North Africa and Central and Eastern Europe. A millennium of jihad (from the seventh century to 1683) brought vast Christian territories and their populations under Islamic rule, transforming Christian civilisations into Islamic ones in Turkey, the Middle East and North Africa. The capital of present-day Turkey, Istanbul, used to be Constantinople, the city of Constantine, the first Roman Emperor to convert to Christianity in the fourth century. The Christian kingdoms of Armenia, Byzantium, Bulgaria, Serbia, Bosnia, Herzegovina, Croatia,

---

[8] 'Engagement: Abidjan 1969', AACC Report on its Second Assembly in Abidjan, 1969: 117.

Albania and parts of Poland and Hungary were conquered. In many of these places, churches were turned into mosques. What is today known as the Umayyad Mosque in Damascus, Syria, used to be the Cathedral of St John the Baptist, and his tomb is still located there.

There are various reasons for the taking over of previously Christian lands by Islam. But the main cause of the dwindling of Christian communities in these territories is that traditional Islam has been associated with socio-political and juridical measures that discriminate against Christians and Jews. These groups have faced various forms of humiliation, restrictions on their socio-religious, political and legal rights, discrimination and, in extreme cases, violent attacks. Today the pressures remain in various forms and degrees across the Islamic world, resulting in Christians emigrating in great numbers from the Middle East to Western countries, thus further accelerating the total takeover of these previously Christian territories by Muslims. Nazareth and Bethlehem, which were predominantly Christian towns, are now virtually Muslim towns due to the migration of Christians to the West. While this is partly a result of the Arab-Israeli conflict, it is also because the Palestinian Christians in these areas are minorities who are not treated as equals by Muslims Palestinians. Instead, they often endure discrimination, and sometimes even contempt and persecution.

The unashamedly public face of Islam (the minarets, call to prayer, veiling of women, etc) makes the tendency to colonise space very high in Islam. Even in places where there are only a few Muslims, one cannot miss them. One can see, feel and breathe Islam! Moreover, Islamic governments and groups sponsor the building of mosques in many Western cities and African villages where there are very few Muslims. Their motivation is to announce the Islamic presence and lay claim to the public space for posterity. This Muslim advance is helped by the Christian tendency to retreat from the public space by vacating or avoiding Muslim suburbs and communities. People in the West tend to sell their houses and move to other areas whenever Muslims move into their suburbs. Christians in the non-Western world shy away from starting churches in Muslim suburbs. All these attitudes inadvertently contribute to conceding the public space to Muslims.

Political Challenge

Politically, Islam poses a real challenge to Christian civilisation and values. Christians regard religion as a matter of personal faith and view the church's past involvement in and use of temporal power as a serious aberration. Muslims, however, regard any attempt at relegating religion to the private sphere as a violation of Islam. For Muslims, Islam is a complete way of life and there can be no separation between private and public, spiritual and temporal, religion and politics, or church and state. They therefore make every effort to lay claim to the public space from which Christians tend to retreat. Hence, while very few Christians in leadership positions will unashamedly exploit their position to advance their religion, very few Muslims would hesitate to do so.

Muslims believe that the whole world belongs to God and that, as the only true believers, they have the right to rule the public space on his behalf. Consequently they feel entitled to demand their own schools in the West and in Africa and to insist on enforcing Islamic law, regardless of the religious composition of the population. Their acute political awareness in the last few decades is matched by a near total lack of political awareness on the part of Christians (especially in Africa). For instance, while it was common in early post-colonial Africa to have non-Muslim heads of state governing majority Muslim countries and vice versa, it is now almost unthinkable to have a non-Muslim head of state governing a Muslim majority. It is, however, not uncommon for a Christian majority to be governed by a Muslim head of state. Christians certainly have a lot to learn from Islam in this regard!

Theological Challenge

Islam also poses a serious theological challenge to Christianity. Muslim views of Christians and Christianity are founded on Islamic replacement theology. From the beginning of his ministry, Muhammad saw himself as in line with past prophets of the Judaeo-Christian tradition. In the early stages of his mission, he portrayed the Qur'ān as the Arabic version of the Jewish and Christian Scriptures. In later stages, however, Islam was portrayed not just as a continuation but as the culmination of the Judaeo-Christian tradition. Abraham, Moses and Jesus (and his disciples) are portrayed in the Qur'ān as Muslims. Jesus is presented as Muhammad's forerunner, who announced the coming of the final and only universal Prophet who brought the final and perfect revelation. Islam therefore considers itself the true Christianity (and the true Judaism). In other words, just as Christianity sees itself as the fulfilment and replacement of Judaism, so Islam sees itself as the fulfilment and replacement of both Judaism and Christianity. The theological challenge of Islam must, therefore, be taken seriously.

Currently, the trend in theological seminaries is to focus on our Judaeo-Christian heritage. No one disputes that the Jewish history and religious traditions contained in the Old Testament are crucial for Christian self-understanding. Much attention is also paid to African Traditional Religion (ATR), which is also important for African Christians' self-understanding. But despite its growing presence in Africa, Islam is almost always ignored or treated as a footnote in a two- or three-hour lecture at the very end of the course. Yet given the far-reaching implications of recent trends in Africa, I would argue that an understanding of Islam is as crucial, and possibly even more crucial, than an understanding of ATR.

Missionary Challenge

Islam is a missionary religion, and the only religion that poses a serious missionary challenge to Christianity. But at first Muslims were more interested in conquests than in converts, and thereafter, with few exceptions, they did not take the missionary calling of their religion seriously. However, this situation changed as a direct result of eighteenth- and nineteenth-century Christian missionary activities. Muslim missionary activity across the globe has increased. While many Christians in the West have become uneasy about and even averse to missions in post-colonial times, Islamic governments across the world are engaged in aggressive propagation of Islam, especially in Africa, Asia and the West.

Many African Muslim intellectuals, and the Arab-Islamic world in general, believe that European colonialism interrupted the natural spread of Islam leaving them with an unfinished agenda. They thus see their mission in post-colonial Africa as the Islamisation and Arabisation of the Christian and animist South. A former head of state of Sudan, Sadiq al-Mahdi, once declared:

the failure of Islam in the southern Sudan would be the failure of Sudanese Muslims to the international Islamic cause. Islam has a holy mission in Africa and southern Sudan is the beginning of that mission.[9]

Over the last few decades, Arab-Muslim countries and various organisations for the propagation of Islam have done much to promote the Arabic language and culture in sub-Saharan Africa. Anti-Western colonial posturing and policies, economic hardship and the collapse of communism have also contributed to many African leaders seeking new alliances with Islamic countries and organisations. President Ghadhafi of Libya took advantage of this situation and succeeded in converting a few African leaders like Omar Bongo of Gabon and Jean Bedel Bokassa of the Central African Republic (who recanted before falling from power). African countries with Muslim minorities like Uganda, Gabon and Benin are members of the Organisation of the Islamic Conference (OIC) whose stated goals include Islamisation and Arabisation.

One of the key objectives of the OIC is 'to make Islamic culture the basis of educational curricula at all levels and stages'. Some of the strategies adopted to achieve this objective mirror what has historically been the Christian missionary approach. They include financing the establishment of primary and secondary schools, funding departments in universities, setting up special study centres and building universities in Western countries and in Africa for the study of Islam and Arabic language and culture. There is also strong support for the training and funding of missionaries to undertake the propagation of Islam, a strategy always accompanied by donations of Qur'āns and the building of mosques. Scores of African students who convert to Islam are offered scholarships to study in Islamic countries like Egypt, Saudi Arabia, Libya, Sudan, Kuwait and Iran. Graduates return home from these areas with extremely radicalised views that bring them into confrontation with the overwhelmingly moderate majority of the Muslim community as well as with non-Muslims.

If we are to meet these and many other challenges, Christians have to take the study of Islam seriously.

---

[9] Gabriel R. Warburg, 'The Shari'a in Sudan', in J. Voll, *Sudan: State and Society in Crisis* (Bloomington: Indiana University Press): 100.

3

Islam: Its Context, Prophet and Early History

In order to understand contemporary Islam, we need to understand something about the times in which Muhammad lived, the details of his life, and the early history of the religion of which he was the prophet.

The Political Context

Islam emerged in the seventh century AD in the region now known as Arabia. At that time, the area was inhabited by nomadic Bedouin, by other semi-nomadic groups, and by people who were permanently settled in small towns like Ta'if or in cities like Mecca and Medina. Mecca, which was located on flourishing trade routes that ran from north to south and from east to west, was an important commercial centre as well as a centre of pilgrimage.

The various ethnic groups living in Arabia were united by individual alliances, but there was no unity in the area as a whole. Blood-feuds between groups were settled by the ethics of revenge, female infants were often buried alive, and women had little protection.

The region was also affected by the power struggle between the two great world powers of the time: the Byzantine and Persian empires. The Byzantine Empire, with its capital in Constantinople, ruled Asia Minor, Syria, Egypt and south-east Europe. It supported the Ghassanid dynasty in Syria as a buffer state against the Arabs, and had Abyssinia (Ethiopia) and Yemen as protectorates. The Persian Empire stretched from present day Iraq to Afghanistan and was under the Sassanid dynasty. The Persians supported the Lakhmid kingdom of Hira in Iraq as a buffer against the Arabs.

There were constant power struggles and feuds between these two empires and their allies. For example, in 614, the Persians captured Jerusalem from the Byzantine Empire, but the Byzantines recaptured it in 628. Struggles like this exhausted both empires, and Islam emerged in the power vacuum that followed in the 630s.

The Religious Context

The empires were riven with conflict, and so was the Christian church, which was deeply divided on doctrinal issues. Ever since the great councils of Nicaea (325) and Chalcedon (451), the churches in the East had been arguing about the doctrine of the Trinity and the person of Christ. The Council of Chalcedon had insisted that Christ was both fully human and fully divine. The Monophysites, however, emphasised his divine nature and gave the impression that Jesus was not fully human. The Nestorians accepted that Jesus had both a divine and a human nature, but thought that these natures were separate. The Gnostics, convinced that matter was evil, completely denied the incarnation, with some even believing that Jesus had not been crucified. They insisted that salvation depended on an experience of mystical enlightenment.

The Byzantine Empire fiercely supported the stance of the Council of Chalcedon. Thus those who accepted this doctrine were known as Melkites (from *malik*, meaning 'emperor', because they agreed with the emperor). Other groups like the Nestorians in Mesopotamia, the Coptic Monophysites in Egypt and the Jacobite Monophysites in Syria were persecuted as heretics.

In the Persian Empire, Zoroastrianism was the state religion, although the empire also contained Christians (especially Nestorian Christians) and other religious minorities. Traditional religions dominated the Arabian Peninsula, where each ethnic group had its own god and goddess, represented by stones. There were numerous priests and priestesses, diviners and soothsayers, and sacrifices were offered in the form of libations to the spirits of caves, trees, wells and stones. Superstitious rituals were rife, there was a strong belief in fate, and little or no belief in an afterlife.

Mecca was a religious centre. The local god of Mecca, Hubal, was highly venerated in the ancient temple known as the *Ka'bah*, which was surrounded by images of deities representing different ethnic groups.

According to Islamic tradition, there were 360 such images, including statues of Jesus and Mary. Many groups made annual pilgrimage to this site. Three goddesses were also worshipped in Mecca: *al-Manat* (the goddess of fate), *al-Lat* (the goddess of fertility) and *al-Uzza* (the goddess of power). These three goddesses were regarded as the 'daughters of Allah'.

Some Arab groups were moving towards henotheism, that is, the belief that one god or goddess is greater (*akbar*) than all the other deities. There were also a few individuals known as *hanif*, who were monotheists. It is clear that the supreme deity was already called *Allah*, meaning 'the God', for important contracts were sealed by taking an oath in this name and the name is mentioned in pre-Islamic poetry.

The whole of the pre-Islamic era in Arabia is referred to in Islamic terminology as the *Jahiliyya* (Period of Ignorance). The emergence of Islam is seen as the dawn of enlightenment. Nevertheless, many religious rituals and social norms and systems dating from this period were adopted, in some cases adapted, and given new meaning in Islam. These include virtually all the rituals of the pilgrimage performed by Muslims today, as well as the laws on marriage, retaliation, circumcision, slavery, and the observance of a holy month in which fighting is forbidden. Traditional Islamic thought justifies the continuation of some of these practices on the basis that they were practised by Abraham, corrupted by later generations, and then purified and reinstated by Muhammad.

Prior to becoming a prophet, Muhammad was a trader who would often have visited Syria. There he would have encountered another religious group, the Sabians, who had a scripture that they called the Book of Seth. Their religious rites included daily prayer at seven fixed times, with worshippers bowing and prostrating themselves. Five of these times correspond to Muslim prayer times. They also observed a thirty-day fast from dawn to dusk and a *fitr* (breaking the fast at the end of the month). Many aspects of Islam are so close to the religion of the Sabians that the Banu Jadhimah clan of Ta'if and Mecca are said to have announced their conversion to Islam by crying out, 'We have become Sabians.'

Strong and well-organised Jewish communities existed around the big oases of North Arabia such as Khaybar and Yathrib (present-day Medina). There were also individual Jews living in and around Mecca. These Jews were mainly agriculturists and their beliefs were largely defined by the Talmud and Jewish apocrypha. Some Arabs may have converted to Judaism.

Christianity was also present, for several nomadic ethnic groups in the Hajaz (the region around Mecca) had embraced this faith. Yemen in the south had been Christian since the fourth century, and there was a strong Christian community in Najran. The presence of Christian monks in the desert is also well attested in both pre-Islamic and Islamic poetry and traditions. In Mecca itself, most of the Christians were non-Arab foreigners from neighbouring countries. They included slaves from Ethiopia and labourers and traders from Syria. Many of these Christians had settled in Arabia to escape persecution elsewhere. They kept themselves aloof from the Arabs and continued to worship in their own languages. The result was that in seventh-century Arabia, Christianity was basically a foreign religion. It was also a divided religion, torn by the doctrinal divisions and confusion outlined above. Moreover, it was associated with a foreign and oppressive political power that fiercely repressed any beliefs that differed from the orthodox religion of the state.

The view of Christianity as a hostile religion was enhanced in 570, when Abraha, a Christian Ethiopian who was governor of Yemen, mounted an expedition against Mecca. His goal is said to have been the destruction of the Ka'bah. The expedition failed, but the attack by an army that included at least one elephant made a deep impression on the Arabs. The year became known as the Year of the Elephant, and Muslim tradition identifies it as the year of Muhammad's birth.

Muhammad, the Prophet of Islam

Muhammad's life

The account of Muhammad's life that will be given here is the one presented in traditional Muslim sources. In other words, it is the Muslim version of events as recorded by the faithful for the faithful.[1]

Muhammad was born in 570. His father, Abdullah, died before he was born and his mother, Amina, passed away when he was only six. An uncle, Abu Talib, took care of him. A rich widow, Khadija, employed

---

[1] The main source is Alfred Guillaume, *The Life of Muhammad: A Translation of Ibn Ishaq's Sirat Rasul Allah* (Oxford: Oxford University Press, 1955).

Muhammad to take care of her trading business. When he was twenty-five and she was forty, she apparently fell in love with him and they were married. He is believed to have had his call to ministry in 610, when he was forty. He started his public preaching of the worship of one God to the polytheistic society of Mecca in 613. He met with opposition but was shielded by his clan ties, which included an influential uncle and a wealthy wife. These two, however, passed away in 619, leaving him in a vulnerable position in Mecca. Some merchants from Medina invited him to migrate to their town and in 622 he accepted their invitation and escaped to Medina, hotly pursued by his Meccan enemies.

The move from Mecca to Medina is known in Islam as the *hijra* which many scholars now translate as 'emigration'. However, the detailed description in traditional Muslim sources of how Muhammad had to leave Mecca under cover of night, hide in the cave of Thawr and use his young cousin, Ali, as a decoy in order to escape death at the hands of his pursuers suggests that 'emigration' is a euphemism.

The hijra is very significant in Islam, for it is the year of Muhammad's escape, rather than of his birth, call or death, which marks the beginning of the Muslim calendar. This year also marks a division between two phases of his ministry. During the twelve-year period in Mecca (610–622), Muhammad's mission was a preparatory one in which he preached, warned and used peaceful persuasion. But the fulfilment of his mission came during the ten-year period in Medina (622–632), when he established a theocracy in which his religious beliefs were integrated in a political, judicial and military framework. From then on, the situation was the one described by the popular saying that 'in Islam there is no separation between religion and politics.'

In Medina, Muhammad and his followers resorted to the traditional Arab nomadic practice of raiding other groups. Muhammad himself participated in twenty-seven battles and raids. The raids provoked a series of battles with the people of Mecca. Muhammad and his followers won the first major battle, the battle of Badr in 624, but the next year they were defeated at the battle of Uhud. When a third battle loomed in 627, they successfully protected Medina by digging a trench around it, with the result that this battle is known as the battle of Trench. In the wake of this battle, orders were issued for the assassination of a number of Muhammad's opponents. Between six hundred and nine hundred

Jewish men were massacred in Medina, while the Jewish women and children were taken as slaves.

In 630, Muhammad marched on Mecca with ten thousand men and captured the city. He executed a few of his leading opponents and granted a general amnesty to the rest. Two years later, he ordered all idol worshippers in Mecca to surrender their idols and convert to Islam within the next four months, or face attack. This emphasis on surrendering reminds us that the term 'Islam' 'is derived from the root word *slm*, which means 'surrender'. Islam demands complete and total surrender or submission to God's will – there is no scope for personal choice.

Later that same year (632), Muhammad died in the bosom of his beloved wife, Ayisha, leaving the task of consolidating his work to four of his close associates and successors, who are known as the Rightly Guided Caliphs.

Muhammad's significance

The rule of God in every aspect of human life in the world is the overriding concern of Islam. This belief is encapsulated in the Muslim expression *Insha Allah*, or 'God willing'. God does what he wills, and what he wills must come to pass. Nothing good or evil can take place except with his permission, and nothing can stop him from attaining what he wills. God's will, according to Islam, was entirely dictated to Muhammad through the angel Gabriel and carefully preserved in the Qur'ān, the Islamic Scripture. It is only by submitting to God's will as contained in the Qur'ān that one can have peace.

However, submission and surrender to God's will is incomplete, and in fact impossible, without submission and surrender to the authority of Muhammad, the Apostle of God. That is because according to Islam, Muhammad perfectly lived out the will of God and has become the best example for Muslims to emulate (33:21).[2]

In the early days of Islam, submission meant not just surrendering to God's will, but accepting and submitting to the rule of Muhammad in Medina. Many ethnic groups were given ultimatums to surrender to

---

[2] All references to and direct quotations from the Qur'ān are from the translation by M. Pickthall, as contained in *Alim*, CD-ROM (Baltimore, MD: ISL Software Corporation, 1986–2000). References to the Qur'ān are identified by chapter (suras followed by verse(s). 33:21 therefore stands for Qur'ān chapter 33, verse 21.

him; those who failed to do so were subdued by force. In Islam, God is always coupled with Muhammad. To obey, disobey, deny, fight or separate oneself from one of them is to do the same to the other. One must desire, fear, love and be more devoted to them both than to one's family. A Muslim is therefore a person who has surrendered to God's will and decrees in the Qur'ān, and to the prophetic authority or rule of Muhammad. Hence, 'to become a Muslim [is] to become a subject'[3] and to convert from Islam is to commit treason.

It is only in a total surrender or submission to God and Muhammad as his messenger that one can have peace. The world is thus divided into those who have surrendered (believers) and those who have not (rejecters or unbelievers). Because they refuse to submit, non-Muslims inevitably live in perpetual strife. They are a source of corruption and a threat to Muslims, and hence Muslims and non-Muslims should not fraternise.[4] This belief accounts for Muhammad's attitude to the non-believers in Mecca and for the repressive laws against non-Muslims that were introduced by Muhammad's successor, 'Umar.

The Qur'ān insists that Muhammad is an apostle of God and that his prophetic mission is in line with the biblical tradition represented by Abraham, Moses, Noah and Jesus (4:163). It also testifies that all prophets are endowed with the power to perform miracles as signs of their prophethood. However, when Muhammad was challenged to perform a miracle, he offered no miracle except the 'matchless Qur'ān' (29:50–1; 13:7; 17:59). No one else could produce anything that could match the poetic beauty of the Qur'ān, and thus the Qur'ān itself is a miracle. Its production was also a miracle because it refers to Muhammad as *ummi*, which Muslims interpret as meaning that he was illiterate (although many Western scholars dispute this claim). In the Qur'ān, he is the last prophet and the Seal of the Prophets (33:40).

Although Muhammad's life serves as an eternal model for Muslims (33:21), he is a mortal, like all other prophets (48:29). As a mortal, he sins and requires forgiveness (40:55, 47:19). Muslims, unlike Christians who worship Christ, will always say that they do not worship Muhammad. But while Qur'ānic and Islamic orthodoxy insist that Muhammad is a

---

[3] Kenneth Cragg, *The Call of the Minaret* (New York: Oxford University Press, 1956): 142.
[4] See Amir Abdullah, 'Preserving the Islamic identity in the West: Threats and solutions' in *Nida'ul Islam Magazine*, No. 18, Apr.–May 1997. <http://www.missionislam.com/knowledge/preserveident.htm>, accessed Jan. 2007.

mere mortal, Muslim devotion and traditions have made extravagant claims on his behalf. In Muslim traditions, he is surrounded by miracles: a gazelle spoke to him; a palm tree trunk sighed when he no longer leaned against it while preaching; a poisoned sheep warned him not to eat it; a handkerchief with which he had wiped his mouth and hands would not burn in a furnace. Traditions also report his splitting the moon in two; trees, doors and windows bowing down to him; his healing broken limbs with the touch of his hand; his casting out demons and multiplying food through prayer to feed his followers. Others speak of water flowing from between his fingers for his followers to drink and use for ablution, or claim that his companions heard his meals glorifying God while he ate, and that stones used to greet him whenever he passed through the lanes of Mecca.[5]

Whether in West Africa, Turkey or Indonesia, stories about Muhammad's life have permeated popular Muslim thought and poetry, which is full of descriptions of his marvellous attributes and actions. Every detail of his life is attributed to divine permission or command. He is the most favoured intercessor on the day of judgement, and the best and greatest of the prophets. He is regarded as sinless and is referred to as 'the perfect human being'. His name is never uttered or written without an invocation of blessing (*tasliya* – 'May the blessings and peace of Allah be upon him'). As one leading scholar on the subject puts it, 'The *tasliya* has become an essential, sometimes it would seem, *the* essential of the life of salvation and devotion'[6] to Muslim believers. One tradition reports that Muhammad said that anyone who blessed him a thousand times would be rewarded with many things in paradise, including a palace for each blessing.

Muhammad has a total of two hundred and one titles (as compared with ninety-nine for God) and also shares most of the attributes given to God. The names and titles given to him include the Unique, the Only, the Avenger, the Lord, the Perfect, the Deliverer, the Truth, the Apostle of War, Raiser of the Dead, Companion of God, Answerer of Prayer, Strong Refuge, Way of God, Sword of God, Holy Spirit and Key of Paradise.[7]

---

[5] See 'Muhammad' in *Encyclopaedia of Islam CD-ROM Edition* (Leiden: Koninklijke Brill, 1999).

[6] Constance E. Padwick, *Muslim Devotions: A Study of Prayer-Manuals in Common Use* (Oxford: Oneworld Publications, Reprint 2003): 154.

[7] Samuel M. Zwemer, *The Moslem Christ: An Essay on the Life, Character and Teachings of Jesus Christ According to the Qur'ân and Orthodox Traditions* (New York: American Tract Society, 1912).

He is called the pre-existent Light of God (*Nur Muhammadi*) from which God created other souls in his image.[8] He is reported to have said, 'Whoever has seen me, has seen Allah.' He is like God in that any representation of him in the form of drawing or photograph is strictly prohibited. Muhammad Iqbal, a leading twentieth-century Pakistani Muslim mystic and scholar, stressed the importance of the Prophet in his daring statement: 'You can deny God, but you cannot deny the Prophet'.[9]

The picture of Muhammad in Muslim popular traditions and devotion is thus clearly in contravention of the teaching of the Qur'ān and orthodox Islamic theology.

Muhammad's Four Successors: The Rightly Guided Caliphs

The death of Muhammad caught the young Muslim community unprepared and threw it into confusion. Some even had difficulty accepting that he really had died. Dissension arose between different groups claiming the right of succession. Three main contending parties emerged:

- The Hashemites (*Banu Hashim*) were led by Ali, Muhammad's cousin and son-in-law who was married to the Prophet of Islam's only surviving child, Fatima. They were the immediate family of Muhammad and regarded themselves as his rightful successors by virtue of their blood relationship. They were later joined and dominated by non-Arab converts to Islam (*mawali*), mainly Persians who had suffered various types of discrimination at the hands of their Arab co-religionists.

- The Emigrants (*Muhajirun*) were led by Abu Bakr and 'Umar along with their respective daughters, Aisha and Hafsa, who were wives of Muhammad. They were joined by the Helpers (*Ansar*), who were early converts to Islam in Medina. They based their claim on their loyalty to Muhammad.

---

[8] See, Schimmel, Annemarie, *And Muhammad is His Messenger: The Veneration of the Prophet in Islamic Piety* (Chapel Hill NC: University of North Carolina Press, 1985); Michael Nazir Ali, *Frontiers in Muslim-Christian Encounter* (Oxford: Regnum Books, 1987): 130–36.
[9] Cited in Michael Nazir Ali, *Frontiers*: 136.

- The *Quraysh*, under the leadership of Uthman and Abu Sufyan, were the Meccan patricians. They were eleventh-hour converts who wanted to take advantage of Muhammad's death to re-establish their dominance under the cloak of Islam. They stressed the importance of Mecca and their role as its custodians.

The individuals from these parties who rose to power as Muhammad's successors are known as caliphs (anglicised) or *khulafa* (sing. *khalifa*). This Arabic word means 'vicegerent' or 'viceroy'. The same word is used to denote the uniqueness of human beings as vicegerents of God (the Christian equivalent to this idea is the concept that we are created in the image of God). As a title, it is a short form of *Khalifatu Rasulil-lah* (Successor to the Messenger of God, that is, to Muhammad). The first four caliphs, who occupy a special place in Islam, are referred to as *Al-Khulafa-ur-Rashidun* (the Rightly Guided Caliphs) because they are deemed to have faithfully followed the example of Muhammad in leading the Muslim community of which they were the religious, political, military and judicial heads.

Abu Bakr (632–634)

The first of the Rightly Guided Khalifs was Abu Bakr, who is said to have been a merchant who used his wealth to support the cause of Islam. He gave his daughter Aisha to Muhammad in marriage, and she became his favourite wife. After the death of Muhammad, 'Umar lobbied for Abu Bakr to be chosen as the first caliph, arguing that Muhammad himself had nominated Abu Bakr to lead prayers when he was ill.

As caliph, Abu Bakr faced a lot of trouble from groups who wanted to take advantage of Muhammad's death to declare their independence. They refused to pay *zakat* and attacked Muslim tax collectors. Prophets of all kinds appeared, claiming the allegiance of various groups. For example, a man called Musaylima had his own Qur'ān and preached in the name of *al-Rahman* or the Merciful, another name for God in Arabic. Abu Bakr's first task was to subdue these rebellions. He accomplished this with the help of Khalid ibn al-Walid, a skilful and ruthless commander. As a result, Abu Bakr is known as 'the saviour of Islam' and *al-Siddique* (the Righteous One).

Abu Bakr then set out to expand the Islamic domain outside Arabia. He captured southern Iraq in 633 with the help of the Lakhmids, the Arab allies of Persia, and then successfully attacked the Byzantine Empire, with the help of the Arab Ghassanids. This victory opened Palestine to the Muslims.

Muhammad had not left a written copy of the Qur'ān; rather, his words had been committed to memory by some of his followers, who were known as *huffaz* (rememberers). Many of these huffaz died in the battles of Abu Bakr's reign, and so he ordered that the Qur'ān be committed to writing to preserve it.

Before his death on 23 August 634, Abu Bakr nominated 'Umar as his successor.

'Umar ibn al-Khattab (634–644)

'Umar can be called the Paul of Islam. He initially persecuted Muslim converts, but after his conversion he used his wealth to support the cause of Islam. He also gave his daughter Hafsa in marriage to Muhammad. Under 'Umar, Islam expanded rapidly by way of conquests. He captured Damascus with little resistance in 635. There he divided the churches equally between Christians and Muslims, and arranged for one half of the Cathedral of St. John the Baptist to be used as a mosque, while the other half remained a church. This arrangement continued for about eighty years until the whole building was converted into the mosque that is now known as the Umayyad Mosque in Damascus.

'Umar defeated the Byzantines at Yarmuk in 636 and took over all of Syria and Palestine. Jerusalem surrendered and the Christians there were treated with kindness. It is said that when 'Umar visited the Church of the Holy Sepulchre, the church leaders invited him to say his prayers in the church, for it was the time for Islamic prayer. 'Umar declined, explaining that he feared Muslims might use such an action as a pretext to turn the church into a mosque. He therefore offered his prayers outside, on the spot where the Al-Aqsa Mosque stands today.

In the same year, 636, 'Umar captured Mesopotamia from the Persians. Between 640 and 642, his general 'Amr ibn al-'As conquered Egypt and the rest of North Africa. Thus, 'Umar is referred to as 'the second founder of Islam'.

Stories abound of 'Umar's humility and his zeal in carrying out prescribed punishments without fear or favour. He also set in place the various administrative and judicial structures of the empire. He divided the empire into provinces, appointed governors, and set up departments to control the treasury, army and public revenues. He arranged for regular salaries to be paid to soldiers. He is also credited with the expulsion of Christians and Jews from the Arabian Peninsula. A pact known as the Covenant of Umar, which he is said to have authored, spelt out discriminatory and humiliating conditions under which Christians and Jews could live under Islamic rule.

'Umar died in 644 after being attacked by a Christian slave (although some sources say that the slave was Zoroastrian).

Uthman (644–656)

Before his death, 'Umar appointed five or six men who were to select the next caliph from among them. One of these men, Abdul Rahman, withdrew his name from consideration. The others then authorised him to appoint the next caliph. The choice appeared to be between Ali, Muhammad's cousin and son-in-law, and Uthman, the leader of the Quraysh faction. Abdul Rahman chose Uthman to become the third caliph.

Uthman was a wealthy man who used his immense wealth to support the cause of Islam. He had been married to two of Muhammad's daughters, Ruqayya and Kulthum, and as a result was known as the Possessor of the Two Lights. Upon becoming caliph, he appointed some of his close relatives as governors of provinces, the most notable being his cousin Muawiya, whom he made governor of Syria. A weak ruler, Uthman lacked the courage to apply the letter of the law when it affected relatives or prominent personalities.

Uthman's most notable contribution to Islam was his ordering Zaid ibn Thabit, Muhammad's personal secretary, to undertake the second compilation of the Qur'ān. When this was done, all the other versions were destroyed. Thus the authorised version of Uthman, which most Muslims today believe to be the authentic and original Qur'ān as given to Muhammad, was the only one left.

In 656, Uthman was allegedly murdered by disgruntled Egyptian Muslims, apparently for what they saw as his nepotism.

Ali ibn Abu Talib (656–661)

Ali was Muhammad's cousin and adopted son. He married the Prophet's daughter Fatima, who gave birth to two boys, Hassan and Husayn. Ali had been one of the first to convert to Islam and had taken part in almost all the battles fought by Muhammad. He was convinced that he was Muhammad's rightful successor. Thus for six months, he had refused to recognise the appointment of Abu Bakr as the first caliph. But now, after having been denied the caliphate three times, he was finally invited to become caliph after the murder of Uthman in June 656.

Ali promptly removed the governors appointed by Uthman. However, the governor of Egypt and Muawiya, the governor of Syria, refused to leave office or pay homage to him. Muawiya, who was the son of Abu Sufyan (the other leader of the Quraysh faction) and a cousin of Uthman, accused Ali of being reluctant to punish Uthman's murderers.

A rebellion led by Ayisha, the widow of Muhammad, and others of his companions resulted in the first serious Muslim civil war. At the Battle of the Camel, Ali's forces defeated those of Ayisha, who went into battle on a camel. Meanwhile Muawiya persisted in his demands for the punishment of the murderers of Uthman. At the battle of Siffin, Ali's forces clashed with those of Muawiya.

Both parties agreed to resort to arbitration to resolve their differences. However, some of Ali's supporters (later referred to as *Kharijites* or separatists) rejected arbitration and accused Ali of seeking a human solution rather than abiding by the divine injunctions spelt out in the Qur'ān.

The arbitration went in favour of Muawiya. Ali was outraged and returned to his supporters, who demanded he repent for accepting arbitration in the first place. This he refused to do. Instead, he attacked his own supporters and massacred thousands of them, further damaging his credibility.

The battle with Muawiya was suspended and another council was convened. This time the council decided to depose both Ali and Muawiya. But both parties refused to accept this decision. Ali and Muawiya stuck to their positions until a Kharijite murdered Ali in 661 in revenge for the massacre of his compatriots. This left Muawiya as the de facto caliph. Ali's second son, Husayn, later took on the fight for the caliphate, but was unsuccessful and was executed in Karbala in present-day Iraq. These events brought about a permanent split between the supporters of Ali, known as the *Shi'ites* or the party of Ali, and the main Muslim body, the *Sunnis*.

4

Mainstream Muslim Beliefs and Practices

In Islam there is a clear distinction between what constitutes 'faith' or 'belief' (*iman*) and 'works' or 'duties' (*ibadat*). Whereas Christianity teaches that salvation is by grace through faith, Islamic teaching implies that salvation is achieved by faith through works. To be a Muslim, one must believe in God, angels, Scriptures, prophets, the last day (and predestination). One must also observe the following duties or works: witness, prayer, fasting, almsgiving, pilgrimage (and jihad).[1]

Articles of Faith

Belief in God

Belief in God (*Allah*) is the first and central belief in Islam. He is depicted as a sovereign, king, ruler and master who is utterly other than his creation. His transcendent status is encapsulated in the familiar Muslim expression, *Allahu akbar* (God is great).

Idolatry, the worship of more than one God, is strongly condemned for Islam stresses the oneness or unity (*tawhid*) of God. He is **one** and has no partners and no children. Associating anything else with God is an unforgivable sin, referred to as *shirk*. Explaining this key Islamic teaching, Badru Kateregga, a Ugandan Muslim, states:

> Because God is one, no one else can share even an atom of His
> Divine power and authority. God alone possesses the attributes

---

[1] For more details about the topics covered in this chapter, see Ghulam Sarwar, *Islam: Beliefs and Practices* (London: Muslim Educational Trust, 1992); John A. Subhan, *Islam: Its Beliefs and Practices* (Lucknow: Lucknow Publishing House, 1938).

of Divinity. Because God is one and one only, to associate any being with God is a sinful and an infidel act.

Islam makes it clear that God has no son, no father, no brother, no wife, no sister and no daughters ... In His unity, God is not like any other person or thing that can come to anyone's mind. His qualities and nature are conspicuously unique. He has no associates.[2]

The emphasis on the oneness of God means that he is never conceived of as a father. Fatherhood would imply that he has children, which to the Muslim mind implies that he cohabited with a woman in order to produce a child. The Qur'ān asks, 'How can He (Allah) have a child, when there is for Him no consort?' (6:101). In the eyes of Muslims, Christians are committing shirk by referring to Jesus as the Son of God and believing in the Trinity (which, according to the Qur'ān, consists of God, Mary and Jesus – 5:116).

God is merciful, compassionate and loving, but only to believers (Muslims). The New Testament ideas of God's love for the sinner, the lost sheep, the lost coin or the prodigal son are alien to Islam. God is severe, especially with unbelievers, and in the Qur'ān he orders Muhammad to fight them and treat them harshly (9:74; 66:9).

Some Muslims interpret the Oneness of God to mean that because God is One, there can only be one true religion (Islam) and one true community of believers (Muslims). In the Qur'ān, God declares to Muhammad, 'This day have I perfected your religion for you and completed My favour unto you, and have chosen for you as religion AL-ISLAM' (5:3). Again 'whoso seeketh as religion other than the Surrender [Islam] it will not be accepted from him, and he will be a loser in the Hereafter' (3:85).

During a Muslim–Christian debate in Dar es Salaam, one Tanzanian Muslim activist declared that 'there is one God, one people and one religion. It is thus unacceptable that the people in this audience belong to different religions.' Revivalist and conservative Muslim groups take this belief seriously and literally.

---

[2] Badru D. Kateregga and David W. Shenk, *Islam and Christianity: A Muslim and a Christian in Dialogue* (Nairobi: Uzima Press, 1980): 2.

Belief in Angels (Malaika) and Other Supernatural Beings

The second key belief in Islam is belief in supernatural beings, who fall into three categories: angels, jinns and the devil.

Angels

Angels are believed to be created from light and are endowed with life, speech and reason. They neither eat nor drink and have no gender differences, and hence do not procreate. They dwell in heaven and their chief task is praising God, carrying out his orders and interceding for mankind (42:3). Angels mentioned in the Qur'ān include *Jibril* (Gabriel), the angel of revelation (2:91; 66:4); *Mikail* (Michael), the angel in charge of rain and sustenance (2:92); *Israfil*, not mentioned in the Qur'ān, but believed to be the angel who will sound the trumpet at the last day; and *Izrail*, the huge and ugly angel of death (32:11 and 6:93). *Mankar*, 'the unknown', and *Nakir*, 'the repudiating', are two angels who are believed to visit the dead in the grave to interrogate them about their belief in God and Muhammad. *Malik* is said to be the presiding angel of hell (43:77), while *Ridwan* is the angel in charge of heaven.

Two angels are also said to sit on the shoulders of every person, recording their deeds (43:80; 82:10–13). There are also guardian angels who protect believers from danger (6:61; 86:4).

Jinns

Jinns are dealt with in Sura 72 of the Qur'ān. They are said to have been created of smokeless fire (15:27) and to be peaceable by nature. They eat and drink and procreate among their own kind, though sometimes in conjunction with human beings. Good ones are very beautiful or handsome, while evil ones are ugly. Jinns can appear to people in the form of snakes, dogs, cats or human beings, and can appear and disappear at will. Some jinns are Muslim and good, while others are non-Muslim and evil.

Devil

The devil is referred to in Islam as *shaytan* or *iblis*. He is believed to have been one of the angels of God. He disobeyed God by refusing to bow down or prostrate himself before Adam, the first created human. God then cast him down to earth and banned him from the precincts of heaven. Iblis is therefore roaming the face of earth, trying to deceive human beings. He sometimes hides behind the walls of heaven to listen to what is going on there. When he is spotted by the angels, they pelt him with stones, and so his other name is the 'pelted one'.

Belief in Prophets

Two terms are used for prophets in Islam: *nabi* (prophet) and *rasul* (apostle/messenger). Muslims believe that every group of people has at one time or another been sent a prophet of their own kind (16:36). The total number of prophets is believed to be 124,000. The Qur'ān mentions only twenty-eight by name, including Noah, Abraham, Moses and Jesus. Some of the prophets have special titles:

Adam	*Safi u-llah*	the Chosen of God
Noah	*Nabi u-llah*	the Prophet of God
Abraham	*Khalil u-llah*	the Friend of God
Ishmael	*Dhabih u-llah*	the Sacrifice of God
Moses	*Kalim u-llah*	the Converser with God
Jesus	*Kalimat u-llah / Ruh u-llah*	the Word/Spirit of God
Muhammad	*Rasul u-llah*	the Apostle of God

Even though Muslims are warned not to make distinctions between the prophets of God, Muhammad occupies the highest place as the 'Seal of the Prophets' (*Khatam Nabiyin* 33:40). One Muslim writer declares: 'Allah has taught us that Muhammad (PBUH [peace be upon him]) has closed (sealed) the long line of His apostles. Who is able to oppose the Qur'ānic teaching?'[3]

Christian students will observe that those referred to as patriarchs in the Judaeo-Christian traditions, such as Abraham, are regarded in Islam as prophets, while most of the major and minor Old Testament prophets like Jeremiah and Hosea are not accorded any significant place.

---

[3] Kateregga and Shenk, *Islam and Christianity.* 46.

Belief in Scriptures

Belief in divinely inspired books, or Scriptures, is the next fundamental belief in Islam. Muslims believe that God has given holy books to different prophets in the past (2:130; 4:135; 5:47, 70, 72 etc). The main such books are the *Tawrat* (Torah) given to Moses, the *Zabur* (Psalms) given to David, and the *Injil* (Gospel) given to Jesus. All these books are portions of the 'mother of books' (*umm ul-kitab*), which resides in heaven. The Qur'ān, however, is the final chapter of the heavenly book and contains the perfect revelation from God.

Unlike Christianity which came after Judaism but accepted and reinterpreted Jewish Scriptures to suit its own self-understanding, Islam completely rejects previous Scriptures, and in particular the Jewish and Christian Bible. Muslims argue (albeit without any empirical evidence) that these Scriptures have been tampered with, falsified and corrupted by Jews and Christians. Many even insist that the *Gospel of Barnabas* is the original true gospel or injil written by the Apostle Barnabas. This belief is not shaken by the irrefutable proof that this gospel is a work of fiction that was produced in late sixteenth- or early seventeenth-century Spain, or by the fact that it contradicts the Qur'ān by referring to Muhammad, rather than Jesus, as the Messiah. It is also odd that this gospel refers to Jesus as 'Christ' (a title that is the Greek equivalent of the Hebrew 'messiah'), but reports him denying that he is the Messiah.[4] Despite the clear lack of credibility of the so-called *Gospel of Barnabas*, Muslims have translated it into many languages and distributed it around the Islamic world.

This attitude to the Christian Scriptures makes Christian–Muslim dialogue rather unfruitful, for many Muslims reject the Bible and accuse Christians of corrupting it.

Belief in the Last Day (Akhira)

Every Muslim is expected to believe in the Last Day and the Day of Judgement, which is graphically described in Suras 75:1ff; 81:1–19; 82; 83 and 84. This day is variously referred to as *Yaumu l-Qiyamat* (the Day of Resurrection), *Yaumu l-Hisab* (the Day of Reckoning), *Yaumu*

---

[4] Jan Slomp, 'The *Gospel of Barnabas* in recent research', in *Islamochristiana*, Vol. 23 (1997): 81–109.

d-Din (the Day of Judgement) and *As-Sa'a* (the Hour). No one except God knows when it will be (41:47). It will be preceded by signs that will include the appearance of the *Mahdi,* the Rightly Guided One, followed by the second coming of Jesus.

Judgement will then take place by the weighing of deeds, for in Islam salvation has to be earned, whereas in Christianity it is God's gracious gift.. If one's bad deeds outweigh one's good deeds, one will be condemned to hell (*jahanna*). The Qur'ān speaks of a purgatorial hell for Muslims, where after a little suffering they are admitted into heaven (19:72), a blazing fire for Christians (98:5), intense fire for Jews (104: 4) and a huge hot fire for idolaters (2:113).

If one's good deeds outweigh one's bad deeds, one will be admitted to paradise (*janna*). The Qur'ān describes eight paradises in which there are palaces. Each palace contains seventy houses, and in every house there are seventy rooms containing seventy beds, as well as tables and dishes. Milk and wine will flow and the inhabitants will be served by beautiful virgins. The place will be cool and shady and filled with a sweet aroma. All who live there will be preserved at the youthful age of thirty-six, will remain beardless and will suffer no fatigue (4:60; 35:32). They will each be given many wives: 4000 virgins and 8000 previously married women. Above all, they will see God face to face, which is the highest of all rewards.

Belief in Predestination

Though predestination is not always included among the official beliefs of Islam, it is present and very strong in Muslim society. Predestination means that God decrees all things, good and evil, and that nothing happens without his sanction. God has decreed everything in the lives of individuals, including their eternal destination, whether heaven or hell. In his sovereignty, God guides and misguides whomsoever he wills. These decrees are written and preserved on a tablet in heaven and are unchangeable. *Insha Allah,* or God willing, the favourite expression of Muslims, testifies to their belief in the irresistible will and decrees of God.

Duties or Pillars of Faith

Shahadah (Confession of Faith)

The word *shahadah* means to bear witness, attest or certify to something or an event. So when Muslims speak of the Shahadah they are referring to the words with which they testify to their faith in Islam: '*Ashahadah la ilaha illa Allah: Muhammad Rasul Allah*' ('I bear witness that there is no God but Allah, and that Muhammad is the Messenger of Allah').

The words within the Shahadah that are translated as 'there is no God but Allah, and Muhammad is the Messenger of Allah' are known as the *Kalima*, and can be described as the Muslim creed. The Kalima falls into two parts. The first part asserts the Oneness of God (tawhid) by denying the existence or worthiness of all other gods or deities and by affirming the existence or worthiness of the one and only God, Allah. The second part asserts the unique authority of Muhammad within Islam and underscores his status as the last prophet.

Of all the pillars of faith, this alone is absolutely essential. The Kalima is whispered into the ear of a newborn baby and into the ear of a dying Muslim. It should be the first thing one hears upon entering the world and the last thing one hears before leaving the world to meet one's creator.

Salat/Namaz (Prayer)

Salat, or prayer, is obligatory for everyone over the age of twelve and of sound mind. Initially Muhammad and his early followers prayed twice each day, in the morning and evening (11.114). Later on in Medina, they began to pray three times each day (2.238). This change was possibly influenced by the Jews, who prayed three times a day. Eventually Muslims adopted five daily times of prayer, each announced by a *muezzin* who issues the *adhan* or 'call to prayer'. The faithful are summoned to pray at

Salat-az-Subh	Dawn	5.00 a.m.
Salat-az-Zuhr	Midday	12.00 noon
Salat-al-'asr	Afternoon	4.00 p.m.
Salat-al-Maghrib	Evening	6.00 p.m.
Salat-al-'isha	Dusk/Night	8.00 p.m.

Before praying, Muslims must ritually cleanse themselves. *Wudu or wuzu* is the normal ablution. It involves washing certain parts of the body including the mouth, nostrils, ears, private parts, arms and feet. *Ghusul,* a more thorough washing, involves a complete bath and is performed after such things as sexual intercourse or after touching a corpse. If there is no water to wash in, fine sand (*tayammum*) can be used for cleansing.

The *qibla* is the name for the orientation that Muslims must adopt when praying. At one time, Muslims faced Jerusalem, but later it was ruled that they must face Mecca and the *Ka'bah.* There is no truth in the allegation that Muslims pray towards the sun and therefore worship the sun-god.

Prayer can be performed individually, but it is preferable to pray in a group led by a prayer leader (*imam*). The prayers involve adopting prescribed postures and reciting key Qur'ānic verses in Arabic.

Besides these formal prayers (*salat*), there are other non-liturgical prayers such as *du'a* (a prayer of supplication or invocation), *istighf'r* (a prayer of pardon or forgiveness); and *tasb* (a prayer of praise or glorification). These prayers, which are mainly invocations, do not have to be said in Arabic but can be offered in any language.

Zakat (Almsgiving)

The Qur'ān calls on Muslims to give *zakat,* as well as to pray (e.g. 2:43, 271–273). The word zakat means 'to purify', and one purifies one's wealth by giving some percentage of it to the poor and needy. The exact percentage differs depending on the type of possessions one owns. In practice, individuals usually decide on the amount of zakat they will give. However, in Libya and Saudi Arabia, zakat is a part of government taxes.

Muhammad taught his followers to give zakat while he was in Mecca and made it compulsory after the move to Medina. He also made it clear that it was not to be given to his own family, for he was already entitled to a special share of all the booty captured. Rather, zakat is intended to benefit poor Muslims. It may not be given to close relatives, nor to non-Muslims. Thus Muslim non-governmental organisations (NGOs) who get funding from zakat sources are under pressure not to allow non-Muslims to benefit from their services.

In addition to zakat, Muslims can also pay *sadaqa*, a free-will offering given to help the poor. An example of sadaqa is *fitrah*, which is given at the end of Ramadan (2:276).

Saum (Fasting)

The tradition of fasting among Muslims began with Muhammad, who fasted when contemplating in the cave. Initially, he observed Jewish traditional fasts, including the Day of Atonement, and the fasts lasted a full twenty-four hours. However, as his followers became involved in more battles, such long fasts were seen to cause problems. After the Battle of Badr in 624, it was realised that fasting Muslims were too weak to fight their enemies. So the pattern of fasting was changed, and a directive was issued for Muslims to fast from dawn to sunset for thirty days during the month of Ramadan. This month was chosen because legend has it that *Laylat al Qadr*, the Night of Power when the Qur'ān was revealed to Muhammad, was ten days before the end of Ramadan. In honour of this event, the whole Qur'ān should be read during this month. The month is so holy that it is believed that during it the gates of heaven stand open, while those of hell are shut and the devils are chained.

The duty to fast is mentioned in Sura 2:183–87, which prescribes total abstinence from food, drink and conjugal relations during daylight hours in the month of Ramadan. Muslims are also prohibited from taking any medicine or applying any ointment to a wound on the head or to any ear or nose infection. Fasting, like prayer, is compulsory for all over the age of twelve, although those who are travelling, pregnant women, nursing mothers, the sick and the elderly are exempted. They must, however, make up for their failure to fast by fasting at a later date or by giving some offering to the poor.

The end of Ramadan is marked by two days of celebration (known as *id ul-fitr*) and Muslims gather together in the open to say special prayers.

Hajj (Pilgrimage)

Sura 3:96ff specifies that every adult Muslim who is free and physically, mentally and materially able must undertake a pilgrimage to Mecca at least once in his or her lifetime. While most of the rituals surrounding this pilgrimage are rooted in pre-Islamic Arab religion, Islam has invested them with new meanings. The rituals of the pilgrimage all commemorate Abraham's family, and especially the ordeal of Hagar and Ishmael, the great ancestor of all Arabs.

Muslims talk about a great pilgrimage, the *Hajj,* and a lesser pilgrimage, the *Umra*. While the Umra can be performed at any time, the Hajj can only be completed during the month of Dhu l-Hajj, which is the twelfth and last month in the Islamic calendar.

Before entering the *haram* (the sacred area of Mecca), male pilgrims put on special garments known as the *ihram,* which are made of two white sheets. Women put on simple ordinary clothes. From that point on they abstain from shaving or cutting their nails, and from kissing and sex. They go to the Great Mosque of the Ka'bah, which Muslims believe was built by Abraham as the first place of worship. Here they perform the *tawaf* by circling the Ka'bah anticlockwise seven times and touching or kissing it.

After the tawaf the pilgrims go and drink from Zamzam, which is believed to be the spring where Hagar and Ishmael found water. Then they perform the *sa'y*, running or walking briskly seven times between the hills of Safa and Marwa to commemorate Hagar and Ishmael's frantic search for water in the desert after they were driven out of Abraham's home.

The pilgrims then leave Mecca and spend the night in the village of Mina before travelling on to the Plain of Arafat, fifteen kilometres from Mina. There they perform the *wuquf,* which is considered the highpoint of the hajj as they stand and pray for forgiveness of sins.

On their way back to Mina, the pilgrims stop at Muzdalifa, about halfway to Mina, where they spend the night. Each person gathers either forty-nine or seventy pebbles to throw at three stone pillars (*al-jamarat*) in a symbolic attack on Satan. As they approach Mina, each person throws seven pebbles against the first pillar. After this, each person offers a blood sacrifice, either a cow, sheep or camel, and shares with all Muslims worldwide in the festival known as the Feast of Sacrifice (*id ul-adha*). This feast commemorates the time when Abraham offered a ram in sacrifice rather than his son Ishmael (although in Genesis the son is said to be Isaac). Men then shave their heads, take off the ihram and put on normal clothes, and women cut off a lock of their hair. They all return to Mecca and again circle the Ka'bah seven times. The next three days are spent at Mina, where they continue to pray and throw the rest of the stones at the three pillars, seven at each pillar per day. In all, the period of the hajj lasts from the 8th to the 13th day of Dhu l-Hajj. Before leaving, many pilgrims also go to Medina to visit Muhammad's tomb and offer prayers in the Prophet's Mosque (*Al-Masjid al-Nabawi*).

African pilgrims to Mecca are now often sponsored by their governments. This policy was begun by the colonial powers in an attempt to appease Muslims, but today most African governments, including those of countries where Muslims are a very tiny minority, use taxpayers' monies to help Muslims carry out a purely religious duty. The reason may be simple political opportunism on the part of politicians, or they may be responding to pressure from Muslim communities. Many non-Muslims are very unhappy about this sponsorship and it has led to tension, especially in Nigeria. But Muslims should also be concerned. Government sponsorship of pilgrimage opens the door to political interference in and manipulation of a religious duty, and may also undermine the spiritual significance of the act. Going on a pilgrimage was meant to involve personal sacrifice on the part of the pilgrim.

Jihad (Holy War)

Although *jihad* is not normally listed as one of the official duties of a Muslim, it is very much a part of Islam. Etymologically, the word refers to striving or exerting a determined effort to achieve a specific goal. It can be used of the struggle to combat evil and pursue what is good. In other words, it refers to believers striving or struggling 'in the path or cause of God' or 'for the sake of Islam'. However in law, general doctrine and historical tradition, it refers to military action undertaken to expand the cause of Islam or, if need be, defend it.[5] Both these meanings of jihad are referenced by Badru Kateregga, a Ugandan Muslim:

> The struggle in the cause of God is of three kinds. The first is the struggle against a visible [human] enemy. The second is the struggle against the temptation of the devil. The third is the struggle against one's own passions. While carrying on a jihad, Muslims must strive with their time, knowledge, energy,

---

[5] E. Tyan, 'Djihad', in *Encyclopaedia of Islam, CD-ROM Edition* (Leiden: Koninklijke Brill, 1999).

possessions, talents, and all their resources for the cause of God. This is the true meaning of *jihad*, which was commanded by Allah, and expounded by the Holy Prophet, for the faithful to follow. It has a much broader meaning than fighting in battle.[6]

Kateregga's second and third forms of jihad are often spoken of as 'jihad of the heart' or 'spiritual jihad', which means the hatred of evil in all its manifestations, especially in one's own sinful inclinations. However, the 'evils' hated in this form of jihad include non-Muslims and anything that is not Islamic. As one influential Nigerian Muslim intellectual puts it:

> A Muslim is not a person who merely believes, but rather a person who practises Islam and, in addition, hates unbelief, its symbols and men ... A person who, in spite of being a Muslim, fraternizes with unbelievers and innovators and [seeks] worldly benefit from them is, to all intents and purposes, a hypocrite. The people of the Sunna have to keep their distance from those who are the declared enemies of Allah: how can anyone claim to be a lover of Allah if he fraternizes with His enemies?[7]

The Ahmadiyya, an Islamic sect that emerged in nineteenth-century India, especially speak of 'jihad of the tongue', which means speaking out or writing against evil, while Kateregga's first form of jihad is always referred to as 'jihad of the fist' or armed struggle. This form of jihad involves fighting non-Muslims in order to root out evil or vice (non-Islamic values), and establish and promote virtue or good (Islamic values) and then to defend it. Until the late nineteenth century, Muslim jurists used the term jihad purely in this military sense. Armed jihad is enjoined by several verses in the Qur'ān (e.g. 9:5, 6, 29; 4:76–79; 2:186, 214, 215; 8:39–42) and is obligatory for every free male adult Muslim. The Qur'ān warns that in jihad, 'It is not for any prophet to have prisoners until he make wide slaughter in the land' (8:67). One who dies in jihad is considered a martyr and is promised automatic entry into paradise. Muhammad is reported to have said, 'A day and a night of fighting on the frontiers is better than a month of fasting and

---

[6] Kateregga and Shenk, *Islam and Christianity*: 77.
[7] I. Sulaiman, *The Islamic State and the Challenge of History: Ideals, Policies and Operations of the Sokoto Caliphate* (London: Mansell, 1987): 3.

prayer'.[8] The laws governing jihad specify that women, children, the elderly, the disabled and monks are not to be deliberately targeted and killed. Women and children are to be enslaved and taken as booty along with all moveable property.

The doctrine of jihad originates in a form of dualism in Islam, which teaches a perpetual struggle between God and Satan, good and evil, belief and unbelief, Islam and non-Islam, Muslim and non-Muslim. Muslims are believed to be on the side of God and non-Muslims on the side of Satan. Thus all non-Muslims are enemies of God. The Qur'ān declares

> Those who are believers fight in the way of Allah, and unbelievers fight in the idols' way. So fight the friends of Satan; surely the guile of Satan is ever feeble (4:76).

In line with this thinking, the world is divided into *Dar al-Islam* meaning 'the abode of peace or Islam' and *Dar al-Harb* meaning 'the abode of war or non-Islam'. The abode of peace represents areas ruled by Islam and the abode of war represents areas of non-Islamic rule. The two realms will be perpetually at war until Islam eventually triumphs.[9]

Muhammad personally took part in twenty-seven battles and ordered forty-six raids against non-Muslims. Numerous Islamic traditions have him enjoining armed jihad, praising its merits and enumerating the rewards that await martyrs. Here are a few of these, cited from what are regarded by Muslims as authentic or trustworthy Islamic traditions:

> He who when he dies has never campaigned (fought in Holy War) or even intended to campaign dies in a kind of hypocrisy.
>
> Fight against the polytheists with your property, your persons, and your tongues.
>
> The best thing a Muslim can earn is an arrow in the path of God.

---

[8] Cited in Bernard Lewis, *Islam: From the Prophet Muhammad to the Capture of Constantinople*, Vol. 1 (New York: Harper & Row, 1974): 211.

[9] In nineteenth-century India, Muslim scholars debated whether India under British rule, was *Dar al-Islam* or *Dar al-Harb*. Some suggested that since there was freedom of religion under British rule and Muslims could freely practice their faith, India was *Dar al-Amān* (the abode of safety). Muslim minorities in the West also argue that Muhammad's advice to early Muslim converts to seek safety in Christian Abyssinia legitimizes Muslims living under non-Muslim rule, especially when there are dictatorships and rampant abuse of human rights in many Muslim countries.

Every prophet has his monasticism, and the monasticism of this community is the Holy War in the path of God.

Will you not ask me why I laugh? I have seen people of my community who are dragged to paradise against their will. They asked, 'O Prophet of God, who are they?' He said, 'They are non-Arab people whom the warriors in the Holy War have captured and made to enter Islam.'

Swords are the keys of paradise.

In Islam there are three dwellings, the lower, the upper, and the uppermost. The lower is the Islam of generality of Muslims. If you ask anyone of them he will answer, 'I am a Muslim.' In the upper their merits differ, some of the Muslims being better than others. The uppermost is the jihad in the cause of God, which only the best of them attain.[10]

The notion that jihad is a spiritual struggle or a last resort in self-defence is purely a post-modern apologia and is hardly borne out by mainstream Muslim scholarship. On the contrary, Muslims have always taken pride in the military exploits of Muhammad and have written scores of books on these as proof of Muhammad's prophetic mission. A very large portion of Muhammad's biography as written by early Muslim observers deals with battles, raids, plunder, killings and assassinations ordered or carried out by the Prophet of Islam.[11] Quoting from the Bible to prove that the coming of Muhammad is foretold in previous scriptures, Ali al-Tabari, a ninth-century Muslim scholar, referred to Psalm 110 and asked rhetorically:

Who is the one at whose right hand the Lord was, who judged in justice, who cut off heads, and who multiplied dead bodies and corpses, except him [Muhammad] – may God bless and save him – and his nation?'[12]

Writing on military jihad and quoting extensively from the Qur'ān and Muslim traditions, Sheikh 'Abdullah bin Muhammad bin Humaid, ex-chief justice of Saudi Arabia, notes that

[10] Bernard Lewis, *Islam: from the Prophet Muhammad*: 211–12.
[11] See Alfred Guillaume, *The Life of Muhammad*
[12] Ali al-Tabari, cited in Jean-Marie Gaudeul, *Encounters and Clashes: Islam and Christianity in History, Vol. II* (Rome: Pontificio Istituto di Studi Arabi e d'Islamistica, 1984): 220.

at first 'the fighting' was forbidden, then it was permitted and after that it was made obligatory 1) against them who start 'the fighting' against you (Muslims) ... 2) and against all those who worship others along with Allah ... Allah (swt) made 'the fighting' (Jihad) obligatory for the Muslims and gave importance to the subject-matter of Jihad in all the Surah (Chapters of the Qur'ān) which were revealed (at Al-Medina).[13]

Ibrahim Sulaiman, a leading twentieth-century Nigerian Muslim activist, defines jihad as

an ideological war between a believer and an unbeliever, or between a Muslim nation and an unbelieving power, with the sole purpose, from the Muslim's perspective, of either preserving the order of Islam or establishing it.

He argues further:

This struggle should, however, not merely seek to sweep the polytheists from power but should establish the rule of Islam ... The ideal here is a situation in which 'all religions will have perished except Islam'. In addition, Muslims are obliged to continue putting pressure on unbelievers until their false life is weakened beyond recovery.[14]

Disturbing as these words are, they constitute an honest and realistic rendition of the official Islamic teaching on jihad. The worship of anyone other than or along with Allah is enough justification for Muslims to launch a military jihad against the culprits.

Responding to Christian criticism and unease about the sanctioning of war in Islam, the late Ayatullah Morteza Mutahhari of Iran notes that there is a gulf between Islam and Christianity.

If we look closely, we see that in Christianity there is no jihad because it has nothing at all. By which I mean that there is no Christian structure of society, no Christian legal system,

---

[13] Sheikh 'Abdullah bin Muhammad bin Humaid, *Jihad in the Qur'ān and Sunnah,* Muhammad Muhsin Khan [translator from Arabic into English] (Riyadh: Maktaba Dar-us-Salam, n.d.) <www.islamworld.net/index.html>, accessed Nov. 2006.

[14] I. Sulaiman, *Revolution in History: The Jihad of Usman Dan Fodio* (London: G. Mansell, 1986); 120.

and no Christian rules as to how a society is to be formed, for these to contain a law of jihad. There is no substance in Christianity; it contains no more than a few moral teachings ... Islam however is a religion that sees it its duty and commitment to form an Islamic state. Islam came to reform society and to form a nation and government. Its mandate is the reform of the whole world. Such a religion cannot be indifferent. It cannot be without a law of jihad. It came to organize a state, to organize a government. Once this is done, how can it remain without an army? How can it be without a law of jihad?[15]

In practice, idol worshippers have been the target of Muslim jihad, sporadically between the eighth and nineteenth centuries in India, and in a more concerted and organised form in West Africa during the eighteenth and nineteenth centuries. Writing on the necessity of military jihad against believers in African Traditional Religion, a nineteenth-century West African Muslim jihadist exhorted his fellow Muslims:

> Every one of us should fight the infidels nearest to him; we should become one hand against the enemies of Allah, our enemies – the enemies of our ancestors.[16]

Consequently, millions of traditional African believers were slaughtered and tens of millions reduced to slavery in West Africa.[17]

However, it must also be said that there are equally numerous instances in Muslim history in Africa and Asia where idol worshippers were tolerated as subjects in Muslim states for both pragmatic and economic reasons. Yet, despite such instance of tolerance, beliefs about the duty of jihad as outlined above are part of mainstream Muslim teaching. Commenting on the use of military force in Islam, a Muslim writing in the *Australian Muslim Times* in 1991 made it clear that one of the purposes of the use of force is the eradication of polytheism and idolatry.

---

[15] Ayatullah Morteza Mutahhari, *JIHAD: The Holy War of Islam and Its Legitimacy in the Quran* trans. Mohammad Salman Tawhidi, (Tehran: Islamic Propagation Organization, 1985) < http://www.al-islam.org/short/jihad/> , accessed Dec. 2006.

[16] J. R. Willis, *In the Path of Allah – The Passion of Al-Hajj ʿUmar; An Essay into the Nature of Charisma in Islam* (London: Frank Cass, 1989): 176.

[17] See John Azumah, *The Legacy of Arab-Islam in Africa*: Chapter Four

Because Islam does not consider idolatry as a form of religion, but as a deviation, a disease and a myth, Islam perceives that a group of people should not be allowed to tread the path of deviation and myth but that they should be stopped. That is why Islam called the idol-worshippers to the unity of God and if they did not heed there would be recourse to force where the idols would be smashed and the temples destroyed. Islam attempted to prevent any appearance of the elements of idol worship in order to destroy the source of this spiritual and mental disease.[18]

These ideas are well grounded in Islamic Scripture and traditions. We shall therefore proceed to examine the importance of these sources in Islam.

---

[18] S. Hashem Nasserallah, 'Behind misconceptions', *in Australian Muslim Times* (19 Apr. 1991): 9.

5

Scripture (Qur'ān) and Tradition (Hadith)

The two main sources of Islamic teaching are the *Qur'ān*, a name which means 'reciting' or 'recitation', and the *Hadith,* a collection of traditions about what Muhammad did, said or approved. The English translation of a book on the importance of the Qur'ān and Hadith reads, 'The only difference between the Qur'ān and the Hadith is that whereas the former was revealed directly through Gabriel with the very letters that are embodied from Allah, the latter was revealed without letters and words.'[1]

Scripture (Qur'ān)

Muslims describe the 'Qur'ān in the following terms:

> The Qur'ān is the sacred book of the Muslims. It is the last book of guidance from Allah, sent down to Muhammad (pbuh) through the angel Gabriel (*Jibra'il*). Every word of the Qur'ān is the word of Allah. It was revealed over a period of 23 years in the Arabic language, and contains 114 Surahs (chapters) and 6236 verses. Muslims learn to read it in Arabic and many memorise it completely. Muslims are expected to try their best to understand the Qur'ān's meaning and practise its teachings …
>
> The Qur'ān deals with man and his ultimate goal in life. Its teachings cover all aspects of this life and the life after death. It contains principles, doctrines and directions for every sphere

---

[1] *Mishkat al-Masabih, the English translation. Book 1: The importance of the Qur'ān and Hadith:* 2–3.

of human activity. ... The success of human beings on this earth and in the life hereafter depends on obedience to the Qur'ānic teachings.[2]

The Qur'ān has to be recited in Arabic and cannot be translated into another language. Even though translations may be undertaken, the translated Qur'ān will not be accorded the same spiritual and devotional status as the Arabic version. This version is highly venerated by Muslims, almost as if it possesses magical properties. Women are generally discouraged from handling it and men handle it only after undergoing ritual cleansing. No object is ever placed on top of it.

Origin of the Qur'ān

Muslims believe that the Qur'ān was revealed gradually to Muhammad between 610 and 632 from a heavenly document known as the Mother of Books or *umm ul-kitab*. Though Muslims insist that 'every word of the Qur'ān is the word of Allah', the Qur'ān admits that this word was revealed in different ways. At times, Muhammad himself is presented as the author of the words (81:15–21; 84:16–19; 92:14–21); more commonly the words he utters are said to have been recited to him by the angel Gabriel (2:97); and at other times God seems to bypass Gabriel and speak directly to Muhammad (2:252; 3:108; 45:6). When Muhammad received a revelation, he would go into a trance and start to shiver. Then, like the pre-Islamic *kahins* (Arab soothsayers), he would be wrapped up in some garment (73:1–7) apparently to induce new revelations. According to traditional Islamic sources, the words he recited were then memorised by his followers and inscribed on objects such as bones, palm leaves or tree bark. The first words recited by Muhammad are believed to be those in 96:1–5:

> *In the name of thy Lord who createth,*
> *Createth man from a clot.*
> *And thy Lord is the Most Bounteous,*
> *Who teacheth by the pen,*
> *Teacheth man that which he knew not.*

---

[2] Ghulam Sarwar, *Islam: A Brief Guide* (leaflet) (London: Muslim Educational Trust, 1993).

The last words to be dictated, shortly before Muhammad's death, were 5:3:

> Forbidden unto you (for food) are carrion and blood and swine flesh, and that which hath been dedicated unto any other than Allah, and the strangled, and the dead through beating, and the dead through falling from a height, and that which hath been killed by (the goring of) horns, and the devoured of wild beasts, saving that which ye make lawful (by the death stroke), and that which hath been immolated unto idols. And (forbidden is it) that ye swear by the divining arrows. This is an abomination. This day are those who disbelieve in despair of (ever harming) your religion; so fear them not, fear Me! This day have I perfected your religion for you and completed My favor unto you, and have chosen for you as religion AL-ISLAM. Whoso is forced by hunger, not by will, to sin: (for him) lo! Allah is Forgiving, Merciful.

Many of those who originally memorised Muhammad's words died in battle. Consequently the first caliph, Abu Bakr, is said to have instructed Zaid ibn Thabit, Muhammad's personal secretary, to undertake the first compilation of the Qur'ān. This compilation was given to Hafsah, one of Muhammad's widows, for safe keeping. But during the time of Uthman, the third caliph, reports emerged of variant readings or versions of the book in some of the urban centres of the Islamic empire. Hence Uthman appointed Zaid to head a committee that would collect all available copies, decide what was genuine and come out with a standardised copy. Thereafter all variant copies were collected and destroyed.

The text of the Qur'ān at this stage was 'a bare consonantal text, with marks to show verse endings, but no points to distinguish consonants, no marks of vowels, and no orthographic signs of any kind.'[3] It is as if an English text were written with only the consonants, leaving readers to decide which vowels were to be inserted. In the early part of the eighth century, diacritical marks were introduced to resolve differences in regard to syllables, vocalisation and identification of the letters. The

---

[3] Arthur Jeffery, cited by Jane Dammen McAuliffe, *Qur'ānic Christians: An Analysis of Classical and Modern Exegesis* (Cambridge: Cambridge University Press, 1991): 15.

final stabilisation of the Qur'ānic text in 934 is credited to Abu Bakr ibn Mujahid (died 936).

Andrew Rippin, a leading Islamic scholar, thus observes

> the ultimate enshrinement of the text of the Qur'ān as we now know it, understood to be literally the word of God, miraculous, inimitable, linked to an illiterate prophet, and thereby having its authority within the community, was the result of two to three centuries of vigorous debate.[4]

In other words the content of the Qur'ān, as we have it today, underwent lots of discussion and editing for a period of between two and three centuries. Despite this, orthodox Muslims regard 'every letter, word, content, form, and meaning of the Qur'ān [as] Divinely revealed'[5] and argue that

> the Qur'ān is unrivalled in its recording and preservation. The astonishing fact of this book of Allah is that it has remained unchanged even to a letter over the past fourteen centuries.[6]

Content and Structure of the Qur'ān

The Qur'ān is roughly the same size as the New Testament. It has been divided into 114 chapters (known as *suras*): 86 of these are normally identified as having been given to Muhammad while he was in Mecca, and 28 as having been given to him while he was in Medina. The chapters are arranged roughly in order of length, from longest to shortest. Each chapter is further subdivided into verses or *ayats*.

Sura 1, known as the *Fatiha* or 'Opening', is often described as 'the essence of the Qur'ān':

> In the name of Allah, the Beneficent, the Merciful
> Praise be to Allah, Lord of the Worlds,
> The Beneficent, the Merciful:
> Owner of the Day of Judgment,
> Thee (alone) we worship; Thee alone we ask for help.

---

[4] Andrew Rippin, *Muslims: Their Beliefs and Practices*, (London: Routledge, 2001): 32. See also Toby Lester, 'What is the Koran?', in *The Atlantic Monthly* (Jan. 1999) <www.theatlantic.com/doc/prem/199901/koran>, accessed Nov. 2006.

[5] Badru D. Kateregga and David W. Shenk, *Islam and Christianity*: 27.

[6] Ghulam Sarwar, *Islam: A Brief Guide*.

Show us the straight path,

The path of those whom Thou hast favored; Not (the path) of those who earn Thine anger nor of those who go astray.

The Fatiha is as central and important to Muslims as the Lord's Prayer is to Christians. It is recited seventeen times in the course of Muslims' five daily prayers.

Some suras of the Qur'ān are named after biblical figures such as Jonah (10), Joseph (12), Abraham (14) and Mary (19). Several Old Testament stories are also mentioned, including creation (3:189–91; 13:2–4; 31:10–11; 32:4–9), the fall (17:63ff, 38:72–83), Cain and Abel (5:30–36) and Noah and the flood (3:30; 7:57–72; 29:13). There are also a few stories reminiscent of the New Testament, such as the account of the Annunciation (3:45–47). These stories often go beyond the biblical accounts and draw on additional material found in the Jewish Talmud or Midrash and in Syrian and Arabic versions of Christian apocryphal books.

Key Qur'ānic passages have much to say about the nature of God, religion, the laws that should govern many areas of life, the Qur'ān itself, the Bible, Christians and Jesus. Some of these passages are identified in the appendix at the end of this book.

The structure of the Qur'ān is highly repetitive, and individual chapters may deal with a number of unrelated topics. There are also apparent inconsistencies in grammar, law and theology. The verses dating from the early years in Mecca are generally pacifist, peaceful and tolerant, and emphasise the worship of one God, condemn idolatry, proclaim the rights of the oppressed (particularly widows and orphans), warn the wicked and idol worshippers of impending judgment and hell, and promise the righteous paradise. By contrast, the later verses uttered in Medina are militant, political and legalistic. Some appear to endorse or justify judicial and military actions that have already taken place, such as a raid during the traditional holy month of *Rajab* (2:217). Others grant Muhammad special concessions. Thus in 33:50–52 he is allowed to marry more wives than is prescribed in 4:3, and in 33:37 he is permitted to marry the wife of his adopted son, Zaid. Classical Islamic thought refers to the situation which gave rise to these utterances as *asbab ul-nuzul* (occasions of revelations).

The Qur'ān itself acknowledges changes and revisions in its content. It speaks of Muhammad being tempted to make concessions to idol worshippers (17:73); Satan introducing verses (22:52, 53: 19–22); God causing Muhammad to forget some verses (87:6–8); and God deleting or changing recitations (13:39, 16:101, 17:41, 86). A number of conflicting verses can also be found in the Qur'ān. For example, wine is praised in 16:67 and prohibited in 2:219; Christians are praised as being the best friends of Muslims (5:82), and Muslims are warned against having Christians as friends (5:51) since Christians are enemies to be fought (9:29); Christians and Jews will go to heaven (2:62), yet salvation can be found in Islam alone (3:19, 85).

To solve these apparent inconsistencies, the theory of abrogation (*naskh*) was developed. On the basis of 2:106, 16:101 and 22:52, it is argued that where there is a conflict between two or more verses, those recited later supersede those recited earlier. Thus even though there are many peaceful verses in the Qur'ān (regarded as being part of the earlier Meccan recitations), they are annulled by the more intolerant and belligerent verses of the later Medinan recitations. For instance, 9:5 is held to have abrogated more than a hundred peaceful verses in the Qur'ān. This verse, known as the sword verse, reads:

> Then, when the sacred months have passed, slay the idolaters wherever ye find them, and take them (captive), and besiege them, and prepare for them each ambush. But if they repent and establish worship [convert to Islam] and pay the poor-due, then leave their way free. Lo! Allah is forgiving, Merciful.

The Qur'ān and the Bible

The Qur'ān is regarded by Muslims as the word of God dictated to Muhammad. Thus unlike Christians who believe in the *inspiration* of Scripture, Muslims believe in its *dictation*. This fundamental difference is at the root of how both communities understand and interpret their Scriptures. As one leading scholar of Islam put it, 'Muslims come to the Qur'ān asking; what does it say, *not* what does it mean'.

Contrary to what Christians might expect, the closest analogue to the Qur'ān in Christianity is not the Bible but Jesus Christ. Christians regard Jesus as the Word of God made flesh; Muslims regard the Qur'ān as the Word of God made text. Muhammad's role is comparable to that of Mary, the mother of Jesus. Christianity proclaims that God chose to reveal his Son miraculously through a virgin birth; Islam claims that he chose to reveal it through a miraculous revelation to the illiterate Muhammad. To Muslims, questioning the illiteracy of Muhammad is as scandalous as questioning the virginity of Mary is for Christians.

Tradition (Hadith)

The second main source of Islamic teaching is a collection of reports known as the *hadith* (pl. *ahadith*) or traditions. Each hadith contains what is known as a *matn* or *sunna*, which, is a report of something that the Prophet said, did or approved. In other words, the hadith is the report while the sunna is the subject or what is being reported. Because the sunna is contained within the hadith, the two terms have come to be used interchangeably. However, each hadith also contains another part, called the *isnad*, which gives the names of the persons who reported the incident mentioned in the sunna. The isnad can involve a long chain of reporters. For example: 'A told me that B said that C had informed him that D mentioned that he had heard E relate, "I heard F ask the Apostle of God whether …"'.

A Muslim source describes the Sunna in the following terms:

> The Sunna is the example of the Prophet Muhammad (pbuh). It is contained in the books of Hadith, which are collections of the sayings and actions and those actions done with his approval. The Hadith show how to put the Guidance of the Qur'ān into practice. The Hadith were recorded meticulously by the Prophet's companions after his death.[7]

The reason that the Sunna is so important is that every detail of Muhammad's lifestyle is regarded as an eternal example to be emulated, from the way he organised the community in seventh-century Arabia to the way he cut his nails. Gai Eaton, a British convert to Islam, quotes Al-Ghazzali, a leading Muslim mystic and theologian, to the effect that a true Muslim is one who 'imitates the Messenger of Allah in his goings out and his comings in, his movements and his times of rest, the manner

---

[7] Ghulam Sarwar, *Islam: A Brief Guide.*

of his eating, his deportment, his sleep and his speech'. Eaton goes on to say that is why 'a man should sit while putting on his trousers and stand while putting on his turban, start with the right foot when putting on his shoes and, when cutting his nails, begin with the forefinger of the right hand.'[8]

Muslims turn to the Sunna for explanations of obscure verses in the Qur'ān and for guidance on matters about which the Qur'ān is silent. For example, the Qur'ān orders Muslims to pray, but does not specify how they are to pray. This information is derived from the Sunna. Sometimes the Sunna even takes precedence over the Qur'ān. For example, while the Qur'ān prescribes one hundred lashes for adulterers, Muslim law, based on the Sunna, sanctions stoning them to death.

From the second century after the death of Muhammad, people started to invent hadith for their selfish ends, which made the collection and criticism of ahadith the main preoccupation of Muslim scholars. Ahadith therefore came to be classified as spurious (mawdu') or sound (*sahih*). 'Six particular collections have become prominent and are regarded as the most authentic: *Bukhari, Muslim, Tirmidhi, Abu Dawud, Nasa'i and Ibn-i-Majah.*'[9]

---

[8] Gai Eaton, *Islam and the Destiny of Man* (London: George Allen & Unwin, 1985): 187.
[9] Ghulam Sarwar, *Islam: A Brief Guide*.

6

Main Divisions and Movements Within Islam

Within less than three decades of Muhammad's death, the early Muslim community split into two main factions as a result of civil wars during Ali's reign. It is important to note that the divisions in Islam, in contrast to those in Christianity, are rooted in politics rather than dogma. The questions around which the divisions first crystallised were primarily concerned with leadership of the community after the death of the Prophet of Islam. Dogma was always formulated in retrospect to support particular political claims.

Main Divisions

The two main groups that sprang from the political differences were the *Shi'ites* and the *Sunnis*. The Shi'ites faithfully supported Ali's claims to be the rightful successor of Muhammad, whereas the Sunnis remained neutral and were prepared to support Muawiya after the murder of Ali in 661. The latter group were the vast majority and constitute mainstream Islam.

Shi'ites or Shi'a

The Shi'ites were originally known as *shi'at-Ali* (the party of Ali). They regard Ali as the only legitimate successor to Muhammad and see the first three caliphs as usurpers. They believe that Ali, Muhammad's son-in-law, inherited from Fatima part of the divine light believed to be deposited in Muhammad. Thus in their confession of faith, Shi'ites 'testify there is no god but Allah and Muhammad is the Messenger of Allah and Ali is the Friend of Allah.'

Shi'ites regard Ali and particularly his son Husayn as martyrs. Husayn's murder is commemorated on the Day of Ashura (the tenth day of the month of Muharram). On this day, mourners march through the streets in a funeral procession, while beating themselves with all sorts of objects. They endure this pain in order to atone for the cruel murder of the grandson of the Prophet of Islam. The Day of Ashura can be compared with the Christian Good Friday and the Jewish Yom Kippur. Karbala (the place where Husayn was murdered) rivals Mecca as a place of pilgrimage.

Where Sunni Muslims have five pillars of faith (confession, prayer, almsgiving, fasting, and pilgrimage) the Shi'ites have six. Their sixth article of faith is that leadership of the Muslim community is vested in an Imam (leader) who must be a direct descendant of Muhammad and Ali, the first imam. Though not a prophet, the Imam is believed to be divinely inspired, sinless, infallible and the religio-political leader of the community. As the religious guide, he is the final authoritative interpreter of God's will as contained in Islamic law. Shi'ites differ on whether there have been twelve or seven Imams. The *Imamiyya* or Twelvers constitute mainstream Shi'ism, as opposed to the Isma'ilis or Seveners. The Isma'ilis also regard Ali as the incarnated Qur'ān – the 'speaking Qur'ān' – as opposed to the 'corrupt' official Qur'ān of their rivals, the Sunnis. There are also other splinter groups of Shi'ites, some of which consider the Imam to be an incarnation of God and even deify Ali!

All Shi'ites believe that the last Imam (the twelfth for Twelvers and the seventh for Seveners) disappeared and is in hiding. They expect him to return at the end of time to establish peace and justice. The hidden imam communicates through special initiates who speak and act on his behalf.

Shi'ites have their own collection of hadith and their own school of law known as *Al-Ja'fariyya*, founded by Ja'far Al-Hilli (died 1277). They accuse Sunnis of corrupting and changing some parts of the Qur'ān and argue that the 'hidden meaning' of Qur'ānic verses is known only to their Imams and their representatives, who are given the title *ayat-ul-llah* ('sign' or 'representative' of Allah).

Suffering and compassion, martyrdom and sacrifice, atonement and redemption are central components of Shi'ite faith. Ali and his family, along with the Imams, are all models of suffering and sacrifice. Great value is also placed on the intercession of saints known as the 'friends of God'. They are believed to mediate God's grace and blessing to believers.

Shi'ites are mostly found in Iran, Lebanon, Iraq and Pakistan (where there is fierce antagonism between them and Sunnis). The sectarian killings of Sunnis and Shi'ites in Iraq in the wake of the American-led invasion of that country and the toppling of Saddam Hussein in 2003 have much to do with the long-standing antagonism and enmity between the two main divisions of Islam.

Sunnis

The name Sunni derives from the word *Sunna*, which we previously encountered in the discussion of hadith (tradition). The Sunna is the record of the example of the Prophet of Islam, and the Sunnis regard themselves as the true followers of his example. Between 80 and 90 per cent of all Muslims are Sunnis.

Historically, Sunni Islam began with the *Murji'ites* (a name derived from the word meaning 'send back'). These were Muslims who refused to judge or take sides in the conflicts between Ali and Muawiya. As their name implies, they insisted on sending judgement back to God or, in other words, leaving it in his hands. They believed that any sinful Muslim, including the caliph, would be punished in the hereafter. They also rejected the Kharijites' extremist view that the commission of a serious sin renders a Muslim an infidel and therefore a legitimate target of jihad.

Sunnis accept all the first four caliphs (including Ali) as legitimate successors to Muhammad. But they regard the caliphs as political, military and juridical leaders of the community, and not as spiritual leaders as in Shi'a Islam.

Sunnis became preoccupied with the political and legal aspects of Islam. *Fiqh*, the study of Shari'ah law, rather than theology became the hallmark of their scholarship. Four different schools of law emerged:

- the *Maliki school*, founded in Medina by Malik ibn Anas (died 795), is dominant in North and West Africa;
- the *Hanafi school*, founded in Baghdad by Abu Hanifa (died 767), is now predominant in West Asia (excluding Arabia), Lower Egypt, and Pakistan;

- the *Shafi'i school,* founded in Cairo by Imam al-Shafi'i (died 820), is adhered to in Indonesia and East Africa;
- the *Hanbali school,* founded in Baghdad by Ahmad Ibn Hanbal (died 855), is the strictest and most fundamentalist of all the Islamic law schools and is the official law code of Saudi Arabia.

By the end of the ninth century, Islamic law had taken a definitive shape with the closing of the gate of *ijtihad* (independent reasoning). *Taqlid* (unquestioning obedience) became the norm, and there has been little development since then.

Movements in Islam

Although the two major groupings within Islam are the Sunnis and the Shi'ites, there are also a number of smaller subdivisions and movements. The most important of these are Sufism, the Wahhabiyya Movement and the Ahmadiyya Movement.

Sufism

Sufism is Islamic mysticism. It is not so much a sect within Islam as a mode of religious experience that began as a yearning for the deeper spiritual springs of Islam and personal fellowship with God. In this respect it was a reaction against Sunni Islamic formalism and legalism. It became known as Sufism because the early Muslim mystics wore garments made of *suf* (wool), in imitation of Christian monks. Even though monasticism as an institution is condemned in the Qur'ān (57:27), Christian monks are praised for their devotion and humility (5:85). They thus provided the initial stimulus and inspiration to early Sufis, who adopted an ascetic lifestyle in the belief that worldly materialism and power are impediments to attaining a fulfilling spirituality. Thus Sufis are also referred to by the Arabic word *faqir* (poor) and the Persian word *dervish* (beggar). Poverty was thus a virtue for early Sufis.

Sufis draw their teaching mainly from the Qur'ān, and in particular from verses like 'God is nearer to you than your jugular vein' (50:16) and 'wherever ye turn, there is Allah's face' (2:115). In Sufi teaching, Jesus is a model wayfaring ascetic. Sufis also emphasise that God alone exists and acts. Thus all existence and acts are attributed to him. There is no distinction between good and evil as God is the author of everything. To the Sufis, no one has real free will.

While traditional Islamic teaching does not distinguish between spiritual and temporal matters, Sufism regards these worlds as incompatible. They regard the material world as transient and corrupt. Some have taught that it is like a snake, smooth but deadly, and that from the moment God first looked at his handiwork, he hated it!

The main characteristics of Sufi theology as opposed to Islamic theology are:

- Sufis teach God's nearness to believers, as opposed to mainstream Islamic theology which teaches his absolute transcendence.
- Sufis teach a personal relationship with God as opposed to mechanical observance of the five pillars of Islam. The ultimate aim of this personal relationship is *faana* (self-extinction in God) and complete union with the Divine.
- Sufism teaches the love of God towards believers and their reciprocal love for God, rather than emphasising fear of God or punishment in hell. Sura 5:57 serves as a source of inspiration and justification for the emphasis on love.
- Sufis emphasise *tariqa*, the spiritual path of contemplation, rather than the way of the Shari'ah. They see themselves as travellers in this world, on a journey whose final destination is faana.

In contrast to traditional Islam, Sufism teaches the need for a mediator in the form of a spiritual master and guide known as a *shaykh*. A famous saying has it that 'a believer who does not have a human shaykh has Satan for his shaykh'. The disciple must place himself entirely in the master's hands and become 'like a corpse in the hands of the body-washer'. The master blesses his disciples, intercedes for them, prays for them, and prepares amulets and charms to bring them good luck and protection. Some groups believe that the master prays on behalf of his disciples, absolving them from the need to perform the five daily prayers themselves.

Sufis believe that their shaykhs can perform signs and miracles (*karama*), including sometimes creating things *ex nihilo* (out of nothing). Saints are venerated and their intercession is sought. Pilgrimages are undertaken to saints' shrines and tombs to offer sacrifices, ask for blessings and make pledges.

Sufis organise spiritual meetings (*majalis*) once a week, normally on Friday evenings. The meetings involve *dhikr* (uninterrupted repetition of the names of God), singing and special dances. Some groups inflict pain on themselves, and practise fire-walking, glass-eating and playing with serpents. In some cases, Sufi communal devotions are substituted for the obligatory ritual prayers. Pilgrimages to the tombs of saints replace the pilgrimage to Mecca. When questioned about the hajj, one leading Sufi, Abu Sa'id ibn Abi al-Khayr (died 1089) replied that it was a waste of time to travel so far simply to walk round a stone house (the Ka'bah) when the black stone should rather walk round him!

Sufism has a tendency to absorb elements from other religions and philosophies. For example, the Bektashi Order (established at the end of the fifteenth century in Turkey) has borrowed from Christianity the idea of a sort of communion with the sharing of wine, bread and cheese and the practise of confession to spiritual masters (*babas*). Such syncretism has meant that Sufism across the Muslim world has adopted many extra-Islamic superstitions and practices, which are sometimes corrupt. This trend has been particularly strong since the nineteenth century.

Famous Sufi leaders include

- Al-Hasan al-Basri (died 728), one of the first and most distinguished mystics.
- Rabi'ah al-'Adawiyya (died 801), a famous female mystic who popularised the notions of divine love and intimacy with God in Sufism.
- Husain ibn Mansur al-Hallaj (died 922), crucified for declaring that *ana al-Haqq* (I am the Truth).
- Abu Hamid Muhammad al-Ghazali (died 1111), credited with gaining credibility and acceptability for Sufism within mainstream of Islamic thought.
- Muhyi al-Din Ibn 'Arabi (died 1240), described by one scholar as 'the greatest mystical genius of the Arabs'.[1] He is known for formulating the doctrine of saintship and declared himself the 'Seal of the Saints', the perfect manifestation of the Spirit of Muhammad, the 'Seal of the Prophets'.

Well-known organised Sufi orders in Africa include the *Qadiriyya*, *Tijaniyya*, the *Mouride Order* in Senegal and the Gambia, and the *Salihiyya* and *Shadhiliyya* in East Africa. In some African countries like

---

[1] A. J. Arberry, *Sufism: An Account of the Mystics of Islam* (London: Unwin Paperbacks, 1979): 97.

the Sudan, Sufi orders have acquired great political clout, transforming themselves into political parties.

The Wahhabiyya Movement

Muhammad bin Abdul Wahhab (1703–1792) who founded the Wahhabiyya movement came from Northern Arabia. He studied in Medina and travelled widely in Iraq and Iran. During this time he studied Islamic law, theology and mysticism and became attracted to the teachings of the fourteenth century revivalist Ibn Taymiyya (died 1328). Taymiyya insisted on obedience to the letter of the Qur'ān and Hadith and attacked the veneration of saints and pilgrimages to shrines and tombs.

Around the middle of the eighteenth century, Abdul Wahhab returned to Arabia and began to preach against popular religious practices such as the veneration of saints and their tombs. As a result, he was expelled from his hometown. A local ruler, Muhammad bin Saud (died 1765), offered him refuge, and a militant reformist movement that would subdue large portions of Arabia was set in motion. Wherever they conquered, they imposed their strict interpretation of Islam. By the beginning of the nineteenth century, the Saud family controlled most of what is now known as Saudi Arabia. They managed to take control of Mecca and Medina in the 1920s.

When they captured Saudi Arabia, the Wahhabi missionary-warriors, who called themselves the *Ikhwan* or Brotherhood, attacked and desecrated all tombs, including those of the Prophet of Islam and his early companions, as well as the tombs of Ali and Husayn in Najaf and Karbala, which were revered by Shi'ites. They advocated the destruction of the sacred Ka'bah. The Wahhabi were also vehemently opposed to Sufism. They regarded all Muslims who opposed their teaching as unbelievers and enemies of God who must be fought. They urged a return to the Qur'ān and Sunna, and strove for the strict application of the Shari'ah as it was in the seventh century during the time of Muhammad. Military training became part of Wahhabism as the faithful were trained in warfare as *mujahiddun*. Some were sent to different parts of the Muslim world to help fellow Muslims. Wahhabism, which is the official creed of Saudi Arabia, has since inspired and directly influenced other revivalist movements such as al-Qaida. It remains the ideological world view of many Muslims who may not necessarily describe themselves as Wahhabis.

In Ghana, the Wahhabi brand of Islam is represented by the *Ahl ul-Sunna*, who have had several confrontations with mainstream Ghanaian Muslims in the past few years. As one observer noted, the Ahl ul-Sunna in Tamale, Northern Ghana

> often used a rather aggressive approach in their propagation efforts even towards other convinced [Muslims]. Often they talked of an obligation to wage war against adherents of other [Muslim] sects as well as against non-Muslims, which they described as 'kaffers', infidels, whom they felt a heavy obligation to correct, conquer or weed out.[2]

Similar tension and open confrontation between reformers (as they call themselves) and mainstream traditional Muslims, the majority of whom subscribe to Sufism and its practices, is common in African countries like Nigeria and Sudan.

The Ahmadiyya Movement

The founder of the Ahmadiyya Movement was Mirza Ghulam Ahmad, who was born in a village called Qadiyan in the Indian province of Punjab in about 1835. He had no formal education in either a traditional Muslim *madrasa* or in a Western-style school, but instead studied under private tutors. In the heat of the religious controversies that characterised British India in the late nineteenth century, Ghulam gradually became involved in the public disputations between the Hindu sect known as the Arya Samajists and Christian missionaries. He argued in defence of Islam. In 1888, he claimed that he had received a revelation to invite those who were seekers of truth to pledge allegiance (*bay'at*) to him. The inaugural ceremony of the Ahmadiyya Movement took place at Ludhiana in March 1889.

Ghulam Ahmad claimed to be the *Mujaddid*, the Renewer of Islam believed to be sent by God at the start of every century of the Muslim calendar. He identified himself as the fourteenth Mujaddid. He claimed

---

[2] Annette Haaber Ihle, '*It's All about Morals': Islam and Social Mobility among Young and Committed Muslims in Tamale, Northern Ghana* (Unpublished PhD Dissertation submitted to The Carsten Niebuhr Institute, Faculty of Humanities, University of Copenhagen, Aug. 2003): 144.

he could receive revelations, and was therefore a prophet, that he was an incarnation or spiritual representation (*buruz*) of Muhammad and Jesus, that he was the Neha Kalank Avatar of the Hindus, the Mesio Darbahmi of the Zoroastrians, the Promised Messiah of the Jews and the Promised Mahdi of Islam. As the Promised Messiah, he saw his principal mission as the 'breaking of the cross', that is, bringing an end to Christianity.

Ghulam died in 1908 leaving a body of written works. Six years later, a rift among the leadership split the Ahmadiyya movement into two factions – *Lahoris* and *Qadianis*. The Lahoris have moderated some of Ghulam's claims, but the Qadianis continue to regard him as a prophet who received divine revelations. This claim contradicts orthodox Islamic teaching that Muhammad is the final prophet, and thus the Qadianis have formally been declared heretics. Since 1974, they have been banned from performing the *hajj* in Mecca. Their position in mainstream Islam is similar to that of Jehovah's Witnesses in Christianity.

The following are some of the key Ahmadiyya beliefs:
• Prophecy and revelation continue – God has not stopped speaking.
• Ghulam Ahmad is a prophet who received revelations from God.
• Ghulam is superior to Christ, who was not sinless but merely an ordinary priest. Great emphasis is placed on the teaching that 'Christ, the son of Mary, is forever dead'!
• Ghulam is the 'Promised Messiah' and Mahdi (Jesus) will not return.
• The time for waging jihad by the sword is over; now is the time for jihad by miracles and arguments.

Both Qadianis and Lahoris relish anti-Christian polemic. The Ahmadi theory of the fainting or swooning of Jesus on the cross has been adopted by Ahmed Deedat in much of his anti-Christian writing, which is widely distributed in many African countries.

The Qadianis in particular are very active in Ghana and in East and South Africa. They were invited into Ghana in 1921 by a group of coastal (Fanti) Muslim converts. The membership and leadership of the Ghanaian group is dominated by the Fanti and Asante ethnic groups. The movement has thus come to be known locally as Fanti or Asante Islam, in contrast to Sunni or mainline Islam, which is dominated by Ghanaians of northern extraction and other West African nationals.

7
Islamic Law (Shari'ah)

The Arabic word *shari'ah* means 'path', 'road' or 'way'. It is commonly used by Arabic-speaking peoples of the Middle East to refer to various prophetic religions in their totality. Hence we have such phrases as *Shari'aht Musa* (the law or religion of Moses) or *Shari'aht Masih* (the law or religion of the Messiah). It designates a system of laws or the totality of the message of a particular prophet.

The word occurs only once in the Qur'ān, where God tells Muhammad, 'And now have We set thee (O Muhammad) on a clear road of (Our) commandment; so follow it and follow not the whims of those who know not' (45:18). As this quotation suggests, God is the source of all law and Muhammad is the lawgiver.[1] *Shari'aht Muhammad* is thus the law or religion of Muhammad. It is the path or way Muhammad trod, and consists of the rules and regulations governing the lives of Muslims. In principle, these rules are derived from the Qur'ān and from the Sunna (the record of prophetic example or custom) using *ijma* (consensus) and *qiyas* (analogical reasoning). A Muslim statement about the Shari'ah reads:

> Shari'ah is the code of law for the Islamic way of life which Allah has revealed for mankind and commanded us to follow. The word Shari'ah means a clear straight path or example. Shari'ah, or Islamic law, is the code of conduct for Muslims …It aims towards the success and welfare of mankind both in this life and the life after death.
>
> Shari'ah prescribes a complete set of laws for the guidance of mankind so that Good (*Ma'ruf*) may triumph and Evil (*Munkar*) disappears from society. It provides a clear and

---

[1] N. Calder and M. B. Hooker, 'Shari'ah' in *Encyclopaedia of Islam CD-ROM Edition* (Leiden: Koninklijke Brill, 1999).

straight path which leads to progress and fulfilment in life and
the attainment of Allah's pleasure …

Shari'ah has rules for every aspect of life. It is complete and
perfect, and guarantees us success, welfare and peace in this life
on earth and in the life after death.[2]

The Shari'ah is divine law as opposed to human law. It provides the
pattern of conduct for Muslims in all matters ranging from how to cut
one's nails to how to perform prayers and how to run a state. According
to one Muslim writer, the Shari'ah

instructs man on how he should eat, receive visitors, buy and
sell, slaughter animals, clean himself, sleep, go to the toilet,
lead a government, practise justice, pray, and perform other
acts of *ibadat* [worship].[3]

In Islamic law, all acts are graded into five main categories – mandatory
(e.g. prayer), praiseworthy but not obligatory (e.g. extra prayers),
indifferent or neutral (e.g. travel by foot or on horseback), deplorable
but permitted (e.g. gluttony), and prohibited or *haram* (e.g. eating
pork).

As regards Muslims' personal lives, the Shari'ah prescribes that
Muslim men must grow a beard and wear a turban in emulation of
Muhammad. Muslim women must wear a veil, like Muhammad's wives.
Adult Muslims must pray five times a day, fast and pay *zakat*.

As regards their family lives, the Shari'ah deals with when a marriage
is valid, and whom Muslims may or may not marry (e.g. it deals with
issues of equality in terms of ethnic origin, religion, status and race).
Female Muslims cannot marry close relatives or non-Muslims. The
conditions and procedures for divorce are also laid down.

As regards society, the Shari'ah legitimises and regulates slavery. It
dictates how non-Muslims are to live under Muslim rule and prescribes
the punishments for different crimes and sins. The punishments referred
to as *hadd* are those prescribed by the Qur'ān and hadith. They include
amputation of a thief's hand, eighty lashes for drinking alcohol and a
hundred for fornication, stoning to death for adultery, beheading for
apostasy, and execution for the murder of a Muslim. However, a father is

---

[2] Ghulam Sarwar, *Islam: Beliefs and Teachings* (London: Muslim Educational Trust, 1992): 161.
[3] Kateregga and Shenk, *Islam and Christianity*: 67.

not to be executed for the murder of his son, though a son must die for murdering his father. A Muslim is not to be executed for killing a non-Muslim or a slave, though these must be executed for killing a Muslim. Rulers who are guilty of theft, fornication, adultery and drunkenness are exempt from punishment. Other punishments, referred to as *ta'zir*, are left to the discretion of the imam. The Shari'ah also deals with *qisas* (or retaliation).

The Qur'ān legitimises and seeks to regulate jihad (war). The Shari'ah therefore spells out who is eligible to declare a jihad (the imam), who qualifies as a target of jihad (non-Muslims), who is qualified to take part in jihad (free male adult Muslims), how jihad is to be conducted, how the booty is to be shared, and the reward of martyrdom (paradise).

The Shari'ah as the Solution to the Human Condition

Islam presents God as the originator or creator of the universe, who is therefore its sovereign ruler, king and master. As sovereign, he wills, demands and commands. The proper relationship of humanity to God is that of a slave to his master. All are required to obey and submit to the will of God. The overriding concern in Islam is thus God's demands and human submission. In their relationship with God, human beings are no more than 'helpless puppets'.[4]

Islam perceives the fundamental problem of humanity as ignorance of the will of God, not sin. Human beings need to learn what his will is so that they can distinguish right from wrong or, in other words, distinguish what God permits from what he forbids. This knowledge comes only by revelation. Thus the pre-Islamic period in Arabia is described as *jahiliyya* (the period of ignorance), and the coming of Islam is perceived as ushering in enlightenment or knowledge.

God in his mercy has provided '*hidaayah* (divine guidance) to enable [people] to know the Will of God and to try to live in obedience to it'.[5] This guidance is contained in the Scriptures revealed to prophets, with the Qur'ān providing the final and perfect guidance for the present cycle

---

[4] Isma'il Al-Faruqi, 'The nature of Islamic da'wah', in *Christian Mission and Islamic Da'wah: Proceedings of the Chambesy Dialogue Consultation* (Leicester: The Islamic Foundation, 1982): 41.
[5] Khurshid Ahmad, 'Comments', in *Christian Mission and Islamic Da'wah*: 42.

of human history. Thus, according to Isma'il Al-Faruqi, 'the standpoint of Islam is not an "act of faith", but one of "conviction". It is one of knowledge, of trust in the human power to know.'[6]

The fruit of the knowledge obtained by observing God's law or will through the Shari'ah is good works. The most important of these works is observing the five pillars or duties of Islam. Righteousness (or *ihsan*) is obtained through the performance of these duties, and they are the key to *falah* (success or well-being, both in this world and the next – the Islamic equivalent of salvation in Christianity). Observing the Shari'ah is doing God's will and is therefore as crucial to Muslims as faith in Jesus Christ is to Christians.

Muslims believe that those who accept Islam and gain knowledge of God's will by observing the Shari'ah will live in peace and prosper in this world and the next. On the other hand, those who reject Islam will inevitably live in ignorance and strife. *Da'wah*, the propagation of Islam, is therefore 'an invitation to think' which 'cannot be met with indifference except by the cynic, nor with rejection except by the fool or the malevolent'.[7] Such people must be freed from the bondage of ignorance, by force if necessary. Malicious people who are enemies of Islam, and therefore enemies of God, must be fought. The *umma* (Muslim community) is duty-bound to bring about the actualisation of the divine will on earth.

The Actualisation of God's Will on Earth

Far from being a wholly Muslim affair, the Shari'ah has very clear injunctions specifically aimed at non-Muslims (especially Christians and Jews) who are granted the status of *dhimmis* or 'protected people' in an Islamic state. These injunctions will be dealt with in chapter 9.

Islam teaches that the Shari'ah as recited in the Qur'ān and lived out in the Sunna is intended for the guidance of all mankind. By virtue of its submission to the divine law, the *umma* (the community of God) is described in the Qur'ān as 'the best community that hath been raised up for mankind' and Muslims are entrusted with the duty to 'enjoin

---

[6] Isma'il Al-Faruqi, 'The nature of Islamic da'wah', in *Christian Mission and Islamic Da'wah: Proceedings of the Chambésy Dialogue Consultation* (Leicester: The Islamic Foundation, 1982): 37.
[7] Ibid.: 33–34.

right conduct and forbid indecency' or (as it is commonly phrased) to 'command good and forbid evil' (3:110). Muslims have understood this to mean that it is the duty of the umma to see to the actualisation of the rule of God on earth. This is where the whole concept of Islamic da'wah or 'calling' stems from. Al-Faruqi makes this point when he writes:

> The Muslim is supposedly the person who, having accepted the burden, has set himself on the road of actualisation. The non-Muslim still has to accept the charge. Hence, *da'wah* is necessarily addressed to both, to the Muslim to press forward toward actualisation and to the non-Muslim to join the ranks of those who make the pursuit of God's pattern supreme.[8]

Muslims are required to 'enjoin' or 'command' virtue, good or right conduct (i.e. Islam) and to 'forbid' or 'prohibit' vice, evil and wrong conduct (i.e. non-Islam). As commanders and forbidders, Muslims are to do more than just call others to 'the straight path' (Shari'ah); they are to enforce the will of God on earth. Such enforcement involves coercion, which in turn requires the exercise of some form of authority or power. Mawdudi, an influential twentieth-century Pakistani Muslim thinker, explains the Islamic position in the following words:

> Whoever really wants to root out mischief and chaos from God's earth ... it is useless for him to work as a mere preacher. He should stand up to finish the government run on wrong principles, snatch power from the wrongdoers and establish a government based on correct principles and following a proper system.[9]

This idea springs from the conviction that 'the true law in the custody of the true community is the condition of the true society'.[10] As the 'true' or 'best' community, Muslims are the rightful *khulafa* or vicegerents of God on earth, and as such they have the divine right to exercise authority or power on God's earth. Thus exercising authority is vital if Muslims are to fulfil the mission of Islam. Abubakar Mahmud Gumi, one time Grand Mufti (supreme Islamic judge) of Nigeria, is quoted as

---

[8] Ibid.: 35.
[9] Christian W. Troll, 'Two conceptions of da'wa in India: Jama'at-i Islami and Tablighi Jama'at', in *Archives de Sciences Sociales des Religions* 87 (July–Sept. 1994): 130.
[10] K. Cragg, *The Call of the Minaret*: 142.

having said that for Muslims, 'politics is more important than prayer'.[11] These claims are all in accord with the Shari'ah which explicitly forbids non-Muslims from exercising authority over Muslims. Islam must always rule over non-Islam. In light of Islamic political thought therefore, all non-Muslims in position of power in any part of the world are usurpers. Commenting on Sura 9:29, which sanctions fighting and subjugating Jews and Christians and making them pay the subjugation tax (*jizya*) as a sign of their humiliation, Maududi declared that

> Non-Muslims have been granted the freedom to stay outside the Islamic fold and to cling to their false, man-made ways if they so wish. They have, however, absolutely no right to seize the reins of power in any part of God's earth nor to direct the collective affairs of human beings according to their own misconceived doctrines.[12]

The nature and mission of the umma as enshrined in the Shari'ah can therefore be summarised as follows:
- As those who have submitted to the will of God on earth and are treading 'the straight path', Muslims are the rightful custodians of the divine will and therefore constitute the 'right' or 'perfect' human community.
- As custodians of God's will, the umma is duty bound to 'call' or 'invite' others to 'the straight path', *the* way for the whole of humanity.
- Since the will of God is expressed in decrees and explicated in laws (the Shari'ah), it requires policing and enforcement. As 'commanders' and 'forbidders', the umma assumes the role of God's army and police force on earth.
- Policing and enforcement require the exercise of authority. Muslims are the rightful vicegerents and therefore by divine right must exercise political power on God's earth.

In all this, Muhammad serves as the example par excellence. The Meccan phase of Mohammad's life, where he was merely a preacher and a prophet with a strictly religious mission of warning the people, is regarded in mainstream Islam as preparation for the ideal and normative

---

[11] Interview with Gumi quoted in Allan Christellow, 'Three Islamic voices in contemporary Nigeria', in W. R. Roff (ed.), *Islam and the Political Economy of Meaning* (Berkeley: University of California, 1987): 233.
[12] Mawdudi, Abul A'la. *Towards Understanding the Qur`an: English Version of Tafhim al-Qur`an* (trans. and ed.) Zafar Ishaq Ansari (Leicester: The Islamic Foundation, 1988): 124.

Medina phase. In Medina, Muhammad was a warrior and ruler as well as a prophet, and the Kingdom of God was attained within a political and military framework. It was in Medina that a large body of laws and regulations were formulated to govern the community. These legal codes now form the basis for Islamic law. Muslims therefore find it difficult, if not impossible, to separate church (or mosque) and state or to distinguish 'the things that are Caesar's' from 'the things that are God's'. In other words, they do not distinguish what is religious from what is secular. Muslims generally believe that the Islamic (Shari'ah) state is the embodiment of the rule of God in the world.

A recent example of the effect of these beliefs comes from Kano, Nigeria. There assurances were issued that the Shari'ah would not be extended to non-Muslim neighbourhoods. Yet a few days before the imposition of the Shari'ah, Sheikh Umar Ibrahim Kabo, the chairman of the Council of Ulama in Kano, declared at a press conference that 'the government of Kano State does not reserve any area where the commission of crime is allowed'.[13]

Many leading conservative Muslim thinkers are convinced that Muslims cannot accept secularism and democratic systems of governance, for such systems essentially involve freedom of choice. Writing on freedom of belief within the context of Muslim obligations in jihad, the late Ayatullah Morteza Mutahhari draws a distinction between Western and Islamic understandings of religion:

> To them [Westerners] religion is just this. One person chooses Islam, while another chooses Christianity, another chooses Zoroastrianism, while yet another, is least bothered about all of them ... This is their basic supposition, and between their line of thought and ours, there exists a world of difference ... to us, religion means the *siratul-mustaqim*, the 'straight path' of humanity and being indifferent to religion means being indifferent to the straight path, to the real path of progress, of humanity.[14]

---

[13] Farooq A. Kperogi and Aliyu M. Sulaiman, 'Sharia: Triumph of Kano masses', in *Weekly Trust*, Vol. 3 No. 20 (June 30–July 6, 2000): 7.

[14] Ayatullah Morteza Mutahhari, *JIHAD: The Holy War of Islam*. The Ayatullah is Shi'a and not Sunni. However, while Muslims may be bitterly divided on some issues, Muslim teaching is nearly unanimous when it comes to issues relating to non-Muslims.

He goes on to explain what freedom of choice means in Islam:

> What mankind must have, is freedom of thought. Yet there
> are some beliefs which are not in the least rooted in thought;
> they have their root in the mere dormancy and stagnation of
> the spirit, handed down from generation to generation; they
> are the essence of bondage, so that war fought for the sake
> of eliminating such beliefs is war fought for the freedom of
> humanity, not war fought against it. If a man prays for his
> needs to a self-made idol, then, in the words of the Quran, that
> man is lower than an animal … This person must be forcibly
> freed from the internal chains which shackle him.[15]

In other words, even though belief cannot be instilled in a person by
force, unbelief and its objects can be uprooted by force.

Many Christians will regard the teaching on the Shari'ah as
unacceptable, but it is essential that we grasp why it is so important to
Muslims.

The Shari'ah in African Muslim Discourse

Conflicts between those favouring secular democracy and those wanting
to establish Shari'ah have led to untold suffering for both Christians and
Muslims, especially in Nigeria and the Sudan. There can be no doubt
that many African Muslims are suspicious of or reject secular democracy
and its associated legal systems. Ali Mazrui, a leading African Muslim
intellectual, even writes that secularism is the greatest threat to the
advancement of Islam in Africa.[16]

Muslims who reject secular democracy do so for various reasons.
Some see it as being deliberately imposed on Muslim Africa in order to
undermine the implementation of the Shari'ah. Thus Ibraheem Sulaiman
of the Ahmadu Bello University in Nigeria writes of the British colonial
power waging 'war on the Sharia' with a view to ensuring 'the eventual
ascendancy of secularisation in Nigeria, at all costs'.[17]

---

[15] Ayatullah Morteza Mutahhari, *JIHAD: The Holy War.*
[16] Ali Mazrui, *The Africans: A Triple Heritage* (London: BBC, 1986): 19ff
[17] Ibraheem Sulaiman, 'Sharia restoration in Nigeria: The dynamics and the process'. Paper delivered at the International Conference on Sharia, held at the Commonwealth Institute, London, 14 Apr. 2001 < http://www.shariah2001.nmnonline.net/ibrahim_paper.htm>, accessed Dec. 2006.

Muslim hostility to secular democracy is based not only on conspiracy theories but also on the origins of the concept in the Western European Enlightenment and the fact that it is a legacy of a Western Christian heritage. Ibraheem Sulaiman comments:

> To the extent that secularism was imposed on the people by the same power that imposed Christianity, the two approaches to life can logically be construed as representing the two faces of the same coin: Western Imperialism. Muslims have therefore no reason to accept secular values, or to have any faith in secularism.[18]

Reflecting on the theme of what would constitute an appropriate system of governance in Africa and Asia, Isma'il Al-Faruqi laments:

> It is a real pity that Asians and Africans should yearn after the kind of state which was born out of the intellectual and spiritual movements in Europe beginning with the Reformation and finishing in the nineteenth century Romanticism.[19]

In the Nigerian context, the adoption and implementation of Shari'ah is seen as a way for Northern Nigerian Muslims to assert their cultural identity and set themselves apart from their Christian southern counterparts, thereby insulating themselves from the effects of globalisation and westernisation.[20]

But Muslims' concern about secular democracy has even deeper roots than hostility to imperialism. Writing on what he calls 'the hidden Christian agenda', Ali Mazrui declares that 'the concept of the secular state is itself Christian.'[21] Jesus' words in Matthew 22:21, 'Render therefore to Caesar the things that are Caesar's, and to God the things that are God's', are held (rightly or wrongly) to be the main inspiration for the notion of separation between the spiritual and temporal, between church and state. As explained above, Muslims argue that the system of

---

[18] Ibraheem Sulaiman, 'Islam and secularism in Nigeria: An encounter of two civilisations', in *Impact International*, 10–23 Oct. 1986: 8.

[19] Al-Faruqi, Comments in *Christian Mission and Islamic Da'wah*: 87.

[20] See Ali Mazrui, 'Shariacracy and Federal Models in the Era of Globilization'. Paper delivered at the International Conference on Sharia, held at the Commonwealth Institute, London, 14 Apr. 2001 < http://www.shariah2001.nmnonline.net/ibrahim_paper.htm>, accessed Dec. 2006.

[21] Ali Mazrui, 'African Islam and comprehensive religion: Between revivalism and expansion', in N. Alkali et al. (eds.), *Islam in Africa*: 259.

governance Muhammad inaugurated in Medina, which fused spiritual and temporal power, is divinely sanctioned and the only acceptable system of governance for all time. To quote Sulaiman again:

> This is the eternal, unalterable model – the Sunnah – laid down by the blessed Prophet for all times, and for mankind. It is, moreover, the only acceptable framework for Muslims. Muslims have, therefore, an eternal obligation not merely to live as a religious community, but to set up for themselves a state which will safeguard the interests of all people and enhance their moral integrity; a state where Islamic ideals can be given concrete manifestation.[22]

This belief explains why, like the eighteenth- and nineteenth-century West African jihadists who denounced the socio-political institutions of their time, contemporary Muslim revivalists regard Western-inspired democratic pluralism, which essentially involves choice, as *kufr* (unbelief).

A final reason why African Muslims embrace Shari'ah is that they regard it as essential for the rediscovery and reinstatement of 'Africa's glorious Islamic past', a point that was emphasised at the Islamic conference in Abuja, Nigeria, in 1989 which led to the founding of the Islam in Africa Organisation. They claim that this glorious past was overthrown by Western colonial intervention and the imposition of secular democracy. The past they are referring to is the nineteenth-century jihadist rule of parts of West Africa. Hence the international conference on Shari'ah held in the UK in April 2001 discussed the restoration of the Shari'ah in Nigeria.[23]

To Muslims the Shari'ah is not just a legal, socio-political and economic code; rather, it is part of their history and thus of their identity. On this basis, Muslims contend that Shari'ah is about freedom of religion: it is an integral part of their faith which cannot be compromised. Making the point that freedom of religion is enshrined in the Nigerian constitution, Auwalu Hamisu Yadudu of Nigeria observes:

> section 38 of the 1999 constitution guarantees freedom of religion. A Muslim firmly believes that his submission to the will

---

[22] Ibraheem. Sulaiman, 'Islam and secularism in Nigeria': 9.
[23] <http://www.shariah2001.nmnonline.net>, accessed Dec. 2006.

of Allah is inchoate if he were to choose or be made to follow some part of His, Allah's, injunctions, the personal law, and abandon others, the penal system. The Sharia, defined as the Path which embodies the totality of Islamic guidance, seeks to govern every aspect of a believer's life. Islam, being a complete way of life for the believers, knows not the dichotomy so much flaunted by non-Muslims, especially Christians, that religion is a private affair of the individual. To the best of his belief, therefore, a Muslim conceives of his faith as demanding a total submission to the Sharia. To a Muslim, freedom of conscience and to profess a religion of his choice alone or in company of others amounts to not much if a pre-condition, which by the way may be perfectly acceptable to followers of other religions, is stipulated for him.[24]

Both in the Sudan and Nigeria, Muslims have argued that the Shari'ah will be enforced only in Muslim areas, that is, in the Muslim-dominated northern parts of both countries, and not in areas dominated by non-Muslims. They insist that Christian opposition to the enforcement of Shari'ah is rooted in ignorance of and prejudice against Islam in general and the Shari'ah in particular:

The fear of Christians is understandable. They have not read the Qur'an and Hadith, the sources of Islamic law and seen where Allah and His prophets explicitly enjoined Moslems to ensure that they respect the religious rights of others and to treat adherent of other faiths with kindness and justice unless they commit an aggression against Moslems on account of their faith. Christians have not been allowed to read the history of Islamic states, to know the position of Jews and Christians in the Abbasid and Ottoman Empires, for instance, and to compare this with the position of even 'non-Orthodox' Christians under the system run by the Fathers.[25]

---

[24] Awwalu Hamisu Yadudu, 'Benefits of Shariah and challenges of reclaiming a heritage'. Paper delivered at the International Conference on Sharia (London, 14 April 2001) <http://www.shariah2001.nmnonline.net/ yadudu_paper.htm>, accessed Dec. 2006.
[25] Sanusi, Lamido 'The Sharia: A Moslem intervention' <http://www.nmnonline.net/articles/sharia2.htm>, accessed Dec. 2006.

A Christian Perspective[26]

It has to be admitted that Christians have often responded to the Shari'ah debate with knee-jerk reactions and defensive arguments. As pointed out by Lamin Sanneh, 'the debate as it has been conducted in Nigeria has been a one-sided affair in which Muslims have taken the offensive and Christians have reacted with high-decibel slogans about pluralism and multiculturalism'.[27] Much of the Christian response can be said to be ill-informed and fuelled by prejudice. Non-Muslims' ideas about the Shari'ah tend to be derived more from sensationalist journalism and fear of the 'Islamic threat' than from any knowledge of the Islamic legal code.

However, as Rabiatu Ammah, a Ghanaian Muslim intellectual observes, when it comes to misinformation about the Shari'ah,

> Muslims attitudes have not helped the situation in several cases
> – for example in Nigeria, where the application of Islamization
> seems to be more interested in flogging (especially of women)
> than in creating wealth'[28]

She goes on to say that, as a woman, she is just as concerned about the way the Shari'ah is being implemented.

But can all Christian fears and concerns about the Shari'ah be dismissed as misinformed and baseless? What about their fear that the Shari'ah accords Muslims socio-political and religious superiority over non-Muslims and that the numerous discriminatory edicts in the Shari'ah will relegate them to the status of second-class citizens? Bert Breiner observes that the classical formulation of Islamic law, 'even when properly understood, still seems to the Christian to constitute an intolerable infringement of human rights'.[29] In particular, he refers to the fact that in a Shari'ah state, non-Muslims cannot aspire to key positions that involve exercising authority over Muslims; to the restrictions placed on Christian worship and witness; and to Christians' inequality

---

[26] For a fuller Christian response to the theological assumptions of the Shari'ah, see John Azumah, 'Theological foundations of Shari'a: Christian concerns and reservations', in *Transformation*, Vol. 22 No. 4 (Oct. 2005): 238–50.

[27] Lamin Sanneh, *Piety and Power: Muslims and Christians in West Africa* (New York: Orbis, 1996): 129.

[28] Rabiatu Ammah, 'Building God's peace and justice together', in Michael Ipgrave (ed.), *The Road Ahead: A Christian–Muslim Dialogue* (London: Church House Publishing, 2002): 98.

[29] Bert Breiner, 'A Christian view of human rights in Islam', in CSIC Papers, No. 5 (Apr. 1992): 4.

before the law, as they cannot give evidence in a Shari'ah court. The Muslim argument that the Shari'ah applies only to Muslims does not address these Christian concerns. The problem is particularly acute in West African, where religious communities live side by side and where members of a family unit may belong to different religions. Even the designation of Christians as *dhimmis* (protected people) in Islamic law is offensive to Christians, who insist on equal citizenship, not protection. As far as Christians are concerned, signing on to classical formulations of the Shari'ah is equivalent to agreeing to religious and socio-political subjugation by Muslims.

Christians do not deny that secular democracy has Western Christian roots and is therefore imperialistic; however, they point out that the Shari'ah has Arab-Islamic roots, and is thus equally imperialistic. Why replace one tool of imperialism with another? Moreover, although secularism is a product of Western Christian civilisation, so is the concept of the nation state, which most of the world, including Africa, has now adopted. In other words, the nations we know as Ghana, Nigeria, Sudan, Kenya and South Africa are all products of the Western Christian dispensation. To the Christian mind, insisting on imposing Shari'ah as the basis of governance is like buying a diesel vehicle and insisting on using petrol to run it. It is equivalent to 'putting new wine into old wineskins'! The problem cannot be solved by simply throwing off secular democracy and taking on Shari'ah or vice versa.

The truth is that our current collective African experience is very different from that of both the areas whose systems of governance we are so anxious to import wholesale. In 'Christian' Europe and most parts of North Africa and the Middle East, other religions are represented mainly by immigrant or non-indigenous communities. But Africans live with religious plurality, and here the followers of other religions are blood relations, members of the same ethnic and linguistic groups, and fellow citizens in nations like Ghana, Nigeria and Kenya. Thus the yardstick for measuring any system of governance in Africa should not be where the system originated but rather the ways in which it ensures the equality of all citizens and guarantees full representation and participation in public life in a religiously and ethnically pluralistic society.

Any system that fails to take cognisance of the inherent diversity of the African context or that treats any ethnic or religious group as anything less than full nationals with equal rights and responsibilities is bound to be a recipe for conflict. Thus we have to adopt a critical stance towards what we are offered. Wholesale importation of any system of governance, be it from the West or the East, will only serve to perpetuate Africa's predicament as 'the dumping ground of cultural and ideological ideas'.[30]

Close to the heart of all the passionate discussions is the question of trust – or mutual mistrust.[31] Even if we assume, for the sake of argument, that the Shari'ah is just and fair and will guarantee minority rights as Muslims claim, can we trust the people who will administer it? History is full of people who have failed to live up to the ideals they profess. Non-Muslims cannot trust Muslims not to abuse the privileged position accorded them in the Shari'ah. The poverty and corruption that have become endemic in many African countries heighten the chances of abuse and misuse of a system like the Shari'ah.

This mistrust is compounded in some contexts by the historical experience of non-Muslims under Islamic rule. In the Northern Nigerian and Southern Sudanese contexts, for instance, the period Muslims look back to as 'the glorious Islamic past' evokes memories of discrimination, marginalisation, subordination and slavery among non-Muslims, who are now largely Christian.

There are thus legitimate concerns and fears that have to be taken into account when discussing alternative systems of governance.

Dilemmas and Gaps

Christians must acknowledge that Muslims have a strong case when they argue that secular democracy has Christian roots and goes against the grain of Islamic teaching. It is therefore unfair to impose secular norms and values on them. Muslims are also in the right when they insist that the Shari'ah is an integral part of the Islamic faith, and that denying Muslims the right to fully observe it is equivalent to denying them the freedom of religion enshrined in the constitutions of various African countries.

---

[80] N. Alkali et al. (eds.), *Islam in Africa*: 432.
[81] Bert Breiner, 'A Christian view of human rights in Islam': 7ff.

But it is equally important that Muslims not brush aside the concerns that Christians have raised. As the Sudanese Muslim scholar and legal expert Abdullahi Ahmed An-Na'im points out:

> There is a fundamental tension, for example, between sharia notions of the Muslim umma (the exclusive community of Muslims) and national unity among Muslim and non-Muslim citizens of the modern nation state.[32]

Christians genuinely feel that their religious and socio-political rights would be severely curtailed under a Shari'ah system of governance. Just as Muslims resent having non-Islamic values imposed on them, so Christians resent having Islamic values imposed on them. They are apprehensive about any enforcement of the Shari'ah within a shared geographic space.

Both Christians and Muslims need to move the discussion beyond the 'Western Christian democracy versus Arab-Islamic shariacracy' debate. As currently conducted, this debate involves caricatures of both Shari'ah and secular democracy: Shari'ah is presented as being about amputating limbs and flogging, and secularism is presented as being irreligious, immoral and even anti-religious.[33] But as Archbishop Desmond Tutu observed

> A secular state is not a godless or immoral one. It is one in which the state does not owe allegiance to any particular religion and thus no religion has an unfair advantage, or has privileges denied to others.[34]

An additional complication in the debate is that while both Christians and Muslims are passionate about what they do not want, there is little or no evidence that either side knows what it really does want. Christians do not seem to have any alternative of their own to offer and so tend to seek refuge in support for a secular democracy most know very little about. Similarly many of the Muslims who took to the streets in 2000 chanting for the introduction of the Shari'ah in its entirety in Northern

---

[32] Abdullahi Ahmed An-Na'im, 'Islam and human rights in Sahelian Africa', in D. Westerlund and E. E. Rosander (eds.), *African Islam and Islam in Africa*: 89.
[33] See for instance Lamido Sanusi, 'The Sharia: A Moslem intervention'.
[34] Archbishop Desmond Tutu, Comments in *Constitutional Talk*, official newsletter of the [South African] Constitutional Assembly, supplement to *The Cape Times*, 12 July 1995.

Nigeria had little knowledge of what they were asking for. There was, for instance, very little or no internal discussion on what form of Shari'ah best suits our twenty-first-century West African context. In fact, prior to the introduction of the Shari'ah in Northern Nigerian states, there was hardly any discussion among Muslims about which school of law would be followed, let alone of whether the Shari'ah as contained in the classical formulations should be 'restored' or re-worked, taking into account the unique West African collective experience. One would have thought that these basic questions needed to be resolved before embarking on the drive to enforce the Shari'ah, for as a proverb in Kusaal (my local language) says, 'it makes sense to remove the thorn in one's buttocks so that one can sit to remove the thorn in one's foot'. But as they say in English, 'better late than never'! Muslims now seem to be engaged in that discussion. Ibraheem Sulaiman, who in earlier writings talked about 'the eternal, unalterable model', now realises that

> the key to success lies in how ultimately the Sharia itself is nurtured and applied. What is being done so far is a mere restoration of the corpus of laws and regulations developed several centuries ago. Law, to be effective and relevant, must be a continuous evolution. Therefore, mere restoration of Sharia is not enough, and will never serve any purpose. A process of construction of any system of law similar to the one undertaken by the founders of the early schools of law is the least that can be expected of the Ummah. Any attempt to evade this responsibility by hiding behind the schools of law will fail. This is a different age, a different society and a different world. A different legal process responsive to the peculiarities and unique characteristics of this age, this society and this strange world is an absolute and inescapable necessity. The founders of the schools were merely performing their duties to their society. They never intended to solve the problems of generations yet to come, of which they know nothing, neither did they ever claim that the results of their output were valid for all time. We have to do our duty to our society and our time. While we build on their legacy there must be a recognition that the eventual outcome of our work may almost amount to a new invention, not a replica.

> ... there must be a recognition of the fact that the Sharia is
> first and foremost an idea, even before it is law. The Sharia is a
> scholarly and intellectual process, liable to continuous growth
> and evolution. The scholarly and intellectual dimension of
> the Sharia requires a much greater effort than the drive for its
> implementation.[35]

Internal discussions like those proposed by Ibraheem Sulaiman are crucial for both Christians and Muslims as they search for the appropriate form of governance in West Africa. Each group must ensure that it is properly informed about what it is commending to the other, and each must be properly informed about what the other is offering.

Finally, we need to re-examine the premise of the current debate. Muslims and Christians should not be debating Shari'ah and secular democracy. The question we need to explore together is to what extent we want to rely on the state to enforce matters of faith. Africans are deeply religious, but why and how have the office of the chief and that of the priest been kept separate in traditional societies?

In probing these questions, Muslims and Christians have to bear in mind Ibn Khaldun's advice that believers should be cautious about buying into the simplistic notion that religion and politics belong together, for we risk attempting to 'patch our worldly affairs by tearing our religion to pieces. Thus neither our religion lasts nor the worldly affairs we have been patching.'[36] In the same vein, Lamin Sanneh cautions that 'if religion looks to political power for its ultimate defence, then it will find in that its sole vindication and reward, and, in time, its demise.'[37]

---

[35] Ibraheem Sulaiman, 'Sharia restoration in Nigeria: The dynamics and the process'. Even leading Islamist scholars like Sayyid Qutb of the Muslim Brotherhood of Egypt and Hasan al-Turabi of Sudan have expressed similar views with regards to the Shari'ah.
[36] See Franz Rosenthal, Al-Muqaddimah: *An Introduction to History, Vol. 1* (Princeton: Princeton University Press, 1967): 427.
[37] Lamin Sanneh, *Piety and Power*: 122.

8

Islamic Teaching on Women

The status of woman in Islamic societies is a topic that stirs much debate. It is important to note that Islam includes very positive and liberative teaching about women as well as negative and oppressive teaching.

Positive Teaching about Women

In seventh-century Arabia, Islam undoubtedly accorded much more value and honour to women than the rest of society did. The Qur'ān speaks of men and women as being created from 'a single soul', as a consequence of which men should treat them kindly:

> Be careful of your duty to your Lord Who created you from a single soul and from it created its mate and from them twain hath spread abroad a multitude of men and women (4:1).

Muhammad preached against female infanticide, the cruel treatment of women and female prostitution. He also condemned the forceful inheritance of widows by relatives of deceased husbands:

> O ye who believe! It is not lawful for you forcibly to inherit the women (of your deceased kinsmen), nor (that) ye should put constraint upon them that ye may take away a part of that which ye have given them, unless they be guilty of flagrant lewdness. But consort with them in kindness, for if ye hate them it may happen that ye hate a thing wherein Allah hath placed much good (4:19).

The Qur'ān also decrees that women are legally entitled to a share of any inheritance from their deceased parents:

> Unto the men (of a family) belongeth a share of that which
> parents and near kindred leave, and unto the women a share of
> that which parents and near kindred leave, whether it be little
> or much a legal share (4:7).

Both Muslim men and women will be rewarded by God in the
hereafter:

> And their Lord hath heard them (and He saith): Lo! I suffer
> not the work of any worker, male or female, to be lost. Ye
> proceed one from another. So those who fled and were driven
> forth from their homes and suffered damage for My cause, and
> fought and were slain, verily I shall remit their evil deeds from
> them and verily I shall bring them into Gardens underneath
> which rivers flow. A reward from Allah. And with Allah is the
> fairest of rewards (3:195).

Respect and kindness towards parents in general, and mothers in
particular, is emphasised in the Qur'ān. In 4:15–17, those who show
kindness to their parents, and especially to their mothers, are promised
paradise, while woe is pronounced on those who mistreat their parents.
One famous saying attributed to Muhammad declares that 'Paradise lies
at the feet of the mother'.[1]

The Muslim woman's role in the home is to seek the happiness of her
husband, nurture the physical and spiritual development of her children,
and maintain the honour of the family. Abdullah bin Omar related that,
'The Apostle of God said, "The whole world is valuable; but the most
valuable thing in the world is a good woman."'[2] The well-known Arabic
saying *al-ummu madrasatun* ('the mother is a school'), conveys the
importance of her role.

Husbands and wives are intended to be bound to one another in love
and mercy (30:21) They are to be like garments for each other (2:187),
meaning that each is to give the other warmth, protection, comfort,
and joy.

Husbands are called upon to provide for their wives and treat them
kindly. 'Men are maintainers of women', declares the Qur'ān (4:34).

---

[1] All the traditions cited here are from the six authentic collections of hadith, especially the two
most respected volumes, the *Sahih Bukhari* and *Sahih Muslim*.
[2] From *Sahih Muslim*, cited in William Goldsack, *Selections from Muhammadan Traditions* (Madras:
The Christian Literature Society for India, 1923): 163.

'The best among you is the one who is best towards his wife', says one tradition. Another adds, 'O people, your wives have certain rights over you and you have certain rights over them. Treat them well and be kind to them, for they are your partners and committed helpers.'

In Muhammad's last sermon, he is reported to have told his followers: 'You have a claim on your wives, and your wives have a claim on you.' He did not merely preach this but practised it, for there are many stories relating how Muhammad helped his wives at home.

Negative Teaching about Women

The positive attitude to women in Islam is, however, offset by the fact that Islam also maintains some of the practices and attitudes towards women that prevailed in pre-Islamic Arabian society, including polygamy. After the death of Muhammad's first wife, Khadija, he himself took twelve more wives, as well as concubines. He is said to have married his favourite wife, Aisha, when she was six and to have made love to her when she reached the age of nine. The Qur'ān limits the number of wives a believer may have to four at a time, and gives men the right to divorce, a right denied to women. Muslim men are also permitted to keep as many concubines as they desire. Wives, in the words of the Qur'ān, are a 'tilth' or field for men to use at will (2:223). Muhammad is alleged to have said, 'if a man invites his wife to sleep with him and she refuses to come to him, the angels send their curses on her till morning'.

The Qur'ān declares that 'men are a degree higher' than women (2:223) and accords Muslim men the right to beat their wives if they are rebellious (4:34). A tradition attributed to Muhammad advises Muslim men to 'hang up your scourge (whip) in a place where your wife (or wives) can see it'. In another tradition he is reported to have said; 'If I were to order anyone to prostrate himself before another [in worship], I would order a woman to prostrate herself before her husband.'[3] Women are regarded as inferior and deficient in intelligence and religious observance. A tradition to this effect reports Muhammad as having said to a woman:

> I have seen none lacking in intelligence and failing in religion but (at the same time) robbing the wisdom of the wise, besides

---

[3] In the Tirmidhi collection cited in Goldsack, *Muhammadan Traditions*. 172.

you. Upon this the woman remarked: What is wrong with our intelligence and our religion? He (the Holy Prophet) observed: Your lack of intelligence (can be well judged from the fact) that the evidence of two women is equal to one man, that is a proof of the lack of intelligence, and you spend some nights (and days) in which you do not offer prayer [during menstruation] and in the month of Ramadan (during the days) you do not observe fast, that is a failing in religion.[4]

This supposed deficiency on the part of women is reflected in many areas in Islamic law. Menstruating women are forbidden to say the five daily prayers. The Shari'ah prescribes that two sheep are to be slaughtered at the birth of a baby boy and one at the birth of a girl. In inheritance law, a daughter gets half the share of a son. In an Islamic court the testimony of a woman has half the value of that of a man. Compensation for the murder or injury of a woman is also half that of a man's.

Women face many obstacles. In many Islamic countries they have virtually no independent identity but must always have a male overseer, such as a husband or brother. In Saudi Arabia, for instance, until 2002 the only legal evidence of a woman's existence was the appearance of her name on her husband's identity card; if he was dead, then it had to appear on her brother's card or, if she had no brother, on the card of her closest male relative, even if she scarcely knew him. Until 2006, in Islamic courts in Pakistan, a woman could only prove rape if four adult males of impeccable character witnessed the assault! In Islamic communities in the Middle East and South Asia, women who are suspected of sexual indiscretion are often killed by their husbands or male relatives. Such honour killings are justified by quoting Sura 4:15. A man who kills his wife, mother, daughter or sister for sexual indiscretion or for eloping (both acts that are regarded as bringing dishonour to the family) is either lightly fined or immune from prosecution.

The following excerpt is taken from an Amnesty International report dated 1 September 1999. It vividly describes the situation as regards honour killings of women and girls in Pakistan.

Women in Pakistan live in fear. They face death by shooting, burning or killing with axes if they are deemed to have brought

[4] *Sahih Muslim*, Book 001, No. 0142.

shame on the family. They are killed for supposedly 'illicit' relationships, for marrying men of their choice, for divorcing abusive husbands. They are even murdered by their kin if they are raped as they are thereby deemed to have brought shame on their family. The truth of the suspicion does not matter – merely the allegation is enough to bring dishonour on the family and therefore justifies the slaying …

Every year hundreds of women are known to die as a result of honour killings. Many more cases go unreported and almost all go unpunished. The isolation and fear of women living under such threats are compounded by state indifference to and complicity in women's oppression. Police almost invariably take the man's side in honour killings or domestic murders, and rarely prosecute the killers. Even when the men are convicted, the judiciary ensures that they usually receive a light sentence, reinforcing the view that men can kill their female relatives with virtual impunity. Specific laws hamper redress as they discriminate against women …

Often, honour killings are carried out on the flimsiest of grounds, such as by a man who said he had dreamt that his wife had betrayed him. State institutions – the law enforcement apparatus and the judiciary – deal with these crimes against women with extraordinary leniency and the law provides many loopholes for murderers in the name of honour to kill without punishment. As a result, the tradition remains unbroken … The victims range from pre-pubescent girls to grandmothers. They are usually killed on the mere allegation of having entered 'illicit' sexual relationships. They are never given an opportunity to give their version of the allegation as there is no point in doing so – the allegation alone is enough to defile a man's honour and therefore enough to justify the killing of the woman …

Pakistani women abroad do not escape the threat of honour killings. The Nottingham crown court in the United Kingdom in May 1999 sentenced a Pakistani woman and her grown-up son to life imprisonment for murdering the woman's daughter, Rukhsana Naz, a pregnant mother of two children. Rukhsana was perceived to have brought shame on the family by having a sexual relationship outside marriage. Her brother reportedly strangled Rukhsana, while her mother held her down. Two main factors contribute to violence against women: women's commodification and conceptions of honour ... Women are seen to embody the honour of the men to whom they 'belong', as such they must guard their virginity and chastity. By being perceived to enter an 'illicit' sexual relationship, a woman defiles the honour of her guardian and his family. She becomes *kari* and forfeits the right to life.

In most communities there is no other punishment for a kari but death. A man's ability to protect his honour is judged by his family and neighbours. He must publicly demonstrate his power to safeguard his honour by killing those who damaged it and thereby restore it. Honour killings consequently are often performed openly ... Official claims that women's rights are not understood in backward rural areas ignore the fact that there are many urban honour killings and considerable support for them among the educated. For example, Samia Sarwar's mother, a doctor, facilitated the honour killing of her daughter in Lahore in April 1999 when Samia sought divorce from an abusive husband (see below). Shahtaj Qisalbash, a witness during the killing, reported that Samia's mother was 'cool and collected during the getaway, walking away from the murder of her daughter as though the woman slumped in her own blood was a stranger'.[5]

Women are treated as objects of impurity, seduction and outright evil. To prevent them from tempting men with their bodies, they must be segregated and veiled. Tradition groups women, asses and dogs together as objects that invalidate prayer when they pass in front of a worshipper. Muhammad is alleged to have said, 'I have not left after me any calamity more distressing to man than woman.'[6] According to another tradition Muhammad said, 'If there is an evil omen in anything, it is in the house, the woman and the horse.'[7] He is also reported to have said 'O womenfolk, you should give charity and ask much forgiveness

---

[5] <http://web.amnesty.org/library/Index/engASA330181999>, accessed Dec. 2006.
[6] In *Sahih Muslim* and *Sahih Bukhari*, cited in Goldsack, *Muhammadan Traditions*: 162.
[7] *Sahih Bukhari*, Book 62, Vol. 7, No. 31.

for I saw you in bulk amongst the dwellers of Hell.'[8] Those women who make it to heaven are there mainly as rewards for believing men who are promised numerous beautiful wives and concubines!

A More Liberal View of Women: Theory Versus Practice

When assessing the status of women in Islam, it has to be borne in mind that in the practice and even constitutions of some Muslim countries, women enjoy a high degree of freedom. For instance, women have served as prime ministers and presidents in Pakistan and Indonesia. Muslims normally point to these examples and ask why America and many Western states, which claim to champion freedom and women's rights, have yet to elect women to the highest offices. In Turkey, the wearing of the veil is banned in official gatherings. Polygamy is officially banned in Tunisia. In Pakistan, women are joining the army and rising to higher ranks. Similarly in Libya women form the core of Colonel Ghadaffi's personal body guards. Yet while these are commendable examples, they remain no more than important exceptions to the norm.

Alfred Guillaume, a leading expert on Islam, sums up the Islamic teaching on women in the following words:

> The Qur'ān has more to say on the position of women than on any other social question. The guiding note is sounded in the words, 'Women are your tillage', and the word for marriage is that used for the sexual act. The primary object of marriage is the propagation of children, and partly for this and partly for other reasons a man is allowed four wives at a time and an unlimited number of concubines. However, it is laid down that wives are to be treated with kindness and strict impartiality; if a man cannot treat all alike he should keep to one. The husband pays the woman a dowry at the time of marriage, and the money or property so allotted remains her own. The husband may divorce his wife at any time, but he cannot take her back until she has remarried and been divorced by a second husband. A woman cannot sue for divorce on any grounds,

---

[8] Sahih Muslim, Book 001, No. 0142.

and her husband may beat her. In this matter of the status of women lies the greatest difference between the Muslim and the Christian world … To a Muslim who takes his stand on the law of Islam the gulf is unbridgeable, but in actual practice in the civilized communities of the Muslim world a more liberal view of women's place in human society is gradually coming to the fore.[9]

As one can clearly see, Islamic teaching on women is both positive and negative. The negative, however, has come to predominate and seems to have sealed the fate of women in many Islamic societies, especially in the Middle East where women do not enjoy the same rights as men. The currently fashionable argument that the treatment of women in Muslim societies has nothing to do with Islam and everything to do with culture is not borne out by the facts.

---

[9] Alfred Guillaume, *Islam* (Baltimore: Penguin Books, 1954): 71–72.

9

Islamic Teaching on People of Other Faiths

T hree main religious traditions are known to have existed in Arabia at the time of emergence of Islam in the seventh century: Arab Traditional Religion, Judaism and Christianity. The Qur'ān and the Sunna have much to say about other religions and about the development of Muhammad's attitude towards them, which moves from affirmation and confirmation to correction, criticism and eventually open hostility.[1]

The Qur'ān and People of Other Faiths

Much of the discourse in the Qur'ān consists of exchanges between the *kuffar* (unbelievers, particularly those holding to polytheistic Arab Traditional Religion) and Muhammad. In these exchanges Muhammad condemns idol worship and polytheism, calls for the worship of the One God, warns of the impending doom of those who refuse to listen and promises paradise to those who believe.

Positive Teachings in the Qur'ān

The Qur'ān states that there should be 'no compulsion in religion' (2:256) for 'if Allah so willed He could have made mankind one people' (11:118). Elsewhere it states, 'To each among you Allah has prescribed a law [or religion]' (5:48). From these passages one could say the Qur'ān accepts, affirms, respects and indeed calls for the celebration of religious plurality.

---

[1] For a more detailed treatment of this subject, see John Azumah, 'Minority faiths in Islam', in Mark T. B. Laing (ed.), *The Indian Church in Context: Her Emergence, Growth and Mission* (Delhi: CMS/ ISPCK, 2002).

In the Qur'ān, Jews and Christians are referred to as *Ahl al-Kitab* (the People of the Book). In his early exchanges with the traditional believers of Mecca, Muhammad insisted that he preached the same God as Jews and Christians and often referred to these two groups as adjudicators and possible allies. He drew inspiration from the way biblical figures like Noah and Moses triumphed over their unbelieving antagonists and insisted that his teaching was in line with that of biblical prophets (4:163; 2:136). He argued that the only difference between the Qur'ānic message and earlier revelations was that this revelation was given in Arabic. It was the Arabic version of previous Scriptures like the Tawrat (Torah) given to Moses, the Zabur (Psalms) given to David and the Injil (Gospel) given to Jesus (26:192–7; 46:2; 12:2). Meccans could check the truth of Qur'ānic teaching by comparing it with the teaching of Jews and Christians (26:196–7; 21:7).

The Qur'ān also declares that Jews, Christians, Sabians and 'whoever believes in God and the Last Day and does right' will be saved (2:62; 3:199; 5:69). Christians are commended as Muslims' 'best friends' and the 'nearest in affection' to them (5:82). The Jews are spoken of as favoured people who will be particularly rewarded by God on the last day (2:40; 5:69). Indeed, at the start of his mission Muhammad and his followers, like the Jews, prayed towards Jerusalem.

Negative Teachings in the Qur'ān

But these generally peaceful comments are not the whole picture. When the traditional Arab believers rejected Muhammad' warnings, maligned him and persecuted his followers, his exchanges with them grew increasingly critical and even hostile.

Whereas earlier verses had insisted that the Qur'ān confirms Scripture, later verses insist that, more importantly, it watches and judges previous Scriptures (5:48–9; 35:31). Not only does it reveal clearly what the Jews and Christians have hidden in their Scriptures (5:15), but it abrogates the previous Scriptures (2:106). Muhammad is no longer just one in a series of prophets, he is the last and final prophet who brings the final and perfect revelation. Islam, the perfect and preferred religion of God (5:3), is said to be the only way of salvation (3:19, 85).

Jews are accused of rejecting and slaying previous prophets (3:112, 183–4) and of taking Ezra to be a Son of God (9:30). Jews and Christians are charged with concealing and corrupting their Scriptures (4:46; 5:13). Christians are also condemned for seeing Jesus as the Son of God (9:30) and for worshipping three gods (5:75–6) by taking Mary and Jesus as gods alongside Allah (5:116). Associating anything with God is *shirk*, the unforgivable sin in Islam. Christians and Jews are therefore urged to accept the teaching of Islam (3:64–71). Furthermore, Muslims are warned against having Jews and Christians as friends (5:51), while Jews and idolaters are singled out as the worst enemies of Muslims (5:82).

The Qur'ān begins to refer to the kuffar as the worst enemies of Muslims (5:82), and to sanction war against them. The sword verse orders Muslims to 'fight and slay those who join other gods with Allah wherever you find them; besiege them, seize them, lay in wait for them with every kind of ambush' (9:5). Sura 47:4 tells Muslims, 'When you encounter the unbelievers, strike off their heads, until ye have made a great slaughter among them.' Sura 8:39 urges Muslims to fight unbelievers 'until there is no more tumult or oppression. And there prevail justice and faith in Allah altogether and everywhere'. This hostility was not just directed at polytheists, for Sura 9:29 states, 'Make war upon such of those to whom the scriptures have been given [Jews and Christians] ... until they pay the tribute readily in humiliation.'

Muhammad and People of Other Faiths

The way Muhammad related to people of other religions is very important for understanding official Muslim attitudes to and dealings with non-Muslims. His encounters with Arab traditional believers and with Jewish and Christian in Mecca are taken as the template for Muslim relations with non-Muslims worshippers for all time.

Muhammad and Arab Traditional Believers

Muhammad's warnings of the imminent doom of traditional believers in Mecca did not take concrete form until he was forced to flee to Medina in 622. There his perception of his mission changed, and he and his community came to see themselves as the instruments of divine judgement on unbelievers. The Qur'ān then sanctioned a series of battles and raids, mainly against the kuffar. After battles in 624, 625 and 627, Muhammad and his followers finally triumphed over the Meccans in 630. The capture of Mecca and the destruction of the idols there strengthened their conviction that the Muslim community is the vehicle by which divine punishment is meted out to the infidel.

Muhammad, Jews and Christians

After his arrival in Medina in 622, Muhammad made covenants with various parties, including three Jewish groups: the Banu Qaynuqa, Banu al-Nadir and Banu Qurayza. In a document known as the Constitution of Medina, the Jews were recognised as allies and as part of the same community as the Muslims. They were allowed to practise their religion and were required to support Muslims in war.

Some individual Jews converted to Islam, but the overwhelming majority rejected Muhammad's claims and some apparently made fun of them. Muslim traditions report that the Jewish rabbis showed hostility to Muhammad 'in envy, hatred and malice, because God had chosen His apostle from the Arabs'. They argued and debated with Muhammad with the aim of undermining his claims. Their attitude is said to have annoyed him so much that Muslims were instructed to stop praying towards Jerusalem and instead pray facing Mecca (2:142–5).[2] After the Battle of Badr in 624, Muhammad accused the Banu Qaynuqa group of sympathising with the Meccans. He ordered them to acknowledge him as prophet and become Muslims or face the same fate as the Meccans. They refused and were forced into exile, with no more than one camel-load of personal belongings for each family. Then in 625, after the battle of Uhud, Muhammad accused a second Jewish group, the Banu al-Nadir, of treason. After confiscating all their possessions, he ordered them to leave Medina. Most of them fled to the oasis of Khaybar in northern Arabia. A third Jewish group, the Banu Qurayza, were besieged for twenty-five nights after the Battle of Trench in 627. When they surrendered, trenches were dug and between 600 and 700 (some sources say 800 to 900) men were led out in groups and decapitated. Their women and children, along with their other property, were taken as booty.[3] Muhammad then led a raid on Khaybar in northern Arabia in 628 and the people, most of them Jews, surrendered and pleaded for their lives. Muhammad agreed to let them continue cultivating their lands on condition that they gave half of every harvest to the Muslims.

---

[2] Alfred Guillaume, *The Life of Muhammad*: 239.
[3] Ibid.: 461ff.

This arrangement marked the start of what later became known as the *dhimma* (treaty of protection) and the payment of *jizya* (compensation) by any People of the Book who live in an Islamic state.

The main reliable recorded encounter between Muhammad and Christians was his meeting with a group of about sixty Christians from Najran in south Arabia. They called on him in Medina in 630, apparently to swear allegiance to him and seek his protection, in return for which they would pay the jizya. They apparently had some discussions with Muhammad and disagreed on matters of belief. Nevertheless, he offered them his mosque for their prayers.[4]

After Muhammad's death in 632, the conquest of the Arabian Peninsula was consolidated. Syria was captured by 637, Jerusalem in 640, Egypt in 642 and Persia in 652. Abu Bakr, the first caliph (632–634), is known to have continued Muhammad's policies towards the Jews and Christians. He allowed them to stay on the Peninsula, cultivate their farms, practise their religions and pay the jizya. 'Umar Ibn al-Khattab, the second caliph (634–644), initially continued with this policy, but later expelled all Jews and Christians from the Arabian Peninsula. His action was based on words attributed to Muhammad to the effect that 'Two religions shall not remain together in the Peninsula of the Arabs.'[5] This remains the official policy of Saudi Arabia, where only Islam can be openly practised.

The Shari'ah and People of Other Faiths

The standard reference points for Muslim relations with non-Muslims are the Qur'ānic injunctions in 9:5 and 9:29–31, Muhammad's example as recorded in the Sunna, the Constitution of Medina, and other documents. The teaching from these sources has been codified in the Shari'ah, the body of Muslim law.

---

[4] This mosque and the entire area of the *hijaz* (Mecca and Medina), are now officially closed to non-Muslims. Ayatullah Morteza explains this injunction by referring to 9:28, which he translates to mean 'The idolaters are filth, so they must not approach the *Masjid ul-Haram* [in Mecca]'. Ayatullah Morteza Mutahhari, *JIHAD: The Holy War of Islam and Its Legitimacy in the Quran* < http://www.al-islam.org/short/jihad/> , accessed Dec. 2006.
[5] Guillaume, *The Life of Muhammad*: 525.

The Shari'ah and Traditional Religions

The Shari'ah builds on the idea that followers of traditional religions and idol worshippers are, technically, not to be tolerated under Islam. Thus Muslim relations with these groups are usually discussed within the context of jihad. As legitimate targets of jihad, they must either convert, be enslaved or die. In the eighteenth and nineteenth centuries, many traditional communities in India and Africa suffered this fate. Millions of traditional African believers were slaughtered and tens of millions were reduced to slavery in sub-Saharan Africa.

It has to be said that Muslim history in Africa and Asia also includes numerous instances where idol worshippers were tolerated as subjects of Muslim states for purely pragmatic and economic reasons. This situation has, however, not changed the fate of idol worshippers in the statute books of mainstream Islamic teaching.

The Shari'ah, Jews and Christians

Jews and Christians, the 'People of the Book' were also classified as *Ahl al-dhimma* ('the People of the Covenant'), which is normally taken to mean 'protected people'. During the eighth century, a very important document known as the Covenant of Umar spelled out the conditions under which dhimmis can live under Muslim rule.[6] Their presence is to be tolerated and they are to be allowed to administer themselves according to the laws of their own religious traditions and, subject to certain restrictions, allowed freedom of worship, movement and residence. However, although they can maintain their worship and ways of life and have their own leaders, they are not allowed to keep weapons, nor take part in war or jihad, because they cannot be trusted. Nor can they hold positions in which they have authority over Muslims (3:27, 113; 5:56).

Dhimmis have to pay the *kharaj* (land tax) and the jizya (a poll tax whose name indicates that it is being paid in exchange for their lives). The payment of the jizya is to be accompanied by gestures that underscore their humiliation, such as the dhimmi's bowing to the Muslim ruler and

---

[6] See translation of document in F. E. Peters, *Judaism, Christianity, and Islam: The Classical Texts and Their Interpretation*, Vol. 2 (Princeton: Princeton University Press, 1990): 380–81. The details of the prescriptions which follow are drawn from Bat Ye'or and David Maisel, *The Dhimmi: Jews and Christians under Islam* (Madison, NJ: Fairleigh Dickinson University Press, 1985): 51–67.

allowing himself to be hit on the head (9:29). Their inferior status is also driven home by the rule that they may not ride noble animals like horses and camels, but only donkeys, with the additional requirement that they must dismount whenever they meet a Muslim. They must also observe a special dress code. They are not allowed to observe Muslim dress codes or use Muslim terminology and titles. Their houses and places of worship must be shabbier and smaller than those of Muslims. They may not build new places of worship and must not worship in the open. They may not preach to Muslims, let alone convert them, and must not say anything that may seem disrespectful of Islam in general and of Muhammad in particular. Muslim men are free to marry dhimmi women, but a dhimmi man cannot marry a Muslim woman. Marriage or sex between a Muslim woman and a dhimmi man is punishable by death. Civil and criminal cases involving dhimmis and Muslims are judged according to Muslim law, but dhimmis are not allowed to give evidence against Muslims because their testimony is inadmissible in Muslim courts. Thus they have to hire Muslim witnesses if they wish to defend themselves. The law of retaliation also does not apply equally to Muslims and dhimmis. While a dhimmi can be executed for merely raising a hand against a Muslim, a Muslim who kills a dhimmi faces no more than a fine.

Some Muslim rulers have actually enforced these rules. The rules have also inspired sporadic outbursts of communal violence, directed especially against Jews and Christians. Some of these attacks are fuelled by revivalist Muslim preachers and by anger at the high social standing and prestige of some Jews and Christians in Muslim society. In some cases, popular feelings have actually forced Muslim rulers to implement the prescribed discriminatory policies.

In responding to these policies, we should remember that other medieval systems like the Sassanid Empire in Persia had similar discriminatory codes against minority groups. In 1215 the Fourth Lateran Council of the Roman Catholic Church introduced very similar rules for Jews and Muslims in recaptured territories in the Iberian Peninsula. The difference, of course, is that while virtually every Christian today is likely to express horror that the church ever proposed such draconian measures, the discriminatory policies against religious minorities are still official Islamic teaching.

It must also be remembered that traditional Muslim thinking about non-Muslims was formulated in an environment where Muslims were politically dominant over non-Muslims. This was the case during Muhammad's life and during the first three generations of Muslim history (the *salaf*), when vast non-Muslim territories were conquered. The pre-occupation of Muslim jurists at the time was to work out appropriate arrangements for the vast non-Muslim colonised populations, the *dhimmis*. Not surprisingly, their ideas about relations with non-Muslims were generally inclined towards contemptuous toleration of the weak by the strong. The traditions and legal opinions formulated at this time have, in effect, been canonised.

The literature produced in that period clearly reflects the belief that the process of Islamic domination of non-Islam would continue until, in the not-too-distant future, the whole world would either accept the Islamic faith or submit to Muslim rule. Consequently the question of Muslims living on equal terms with non-Muslims or as subjects under non-Muslim rule hardly arose, and where it did, it received only minor and fleeting attention. This is the legacy bequeathed to contemporary modern Muslims, the majority of whom have come to view it not as describing a particular historical situation but as part of the faith, requiring unquestioning adherence and re-enactment at all times and in all places.[7]

The Contemporary Situation

The vast majority of Muslims living as minority communities in sub-Saharan Africa, the West, India and elsewhere want to live at peace and on equal terms with their non-Muslim relatives, friends and neighbours. The same cannot be said of places where Muslims are in the majority, such as parts of North Africa, the Middle East and South-East Asia. In those countries, non-Muslims' rights are restricted and they experience discrimination, persecution and even violent attacks. This attitude towards non-Muslims cuts across Sunni and Shi'ite lines, and is official state policy in Saudi Arabia, Sudan, Iran and other Middle Eastern and North African countries. Father Samir Khalil Samir, an Egyptian Jesuit and professor at St Joseph's University in Beirut, Lebanon, summarises

---

[7] Fazlur Rahman, *Islam* (Chicago: University of Chicago Press, 1979): 236–37.

the conditions under which the Christian minority live in contemporary Egypt and the Middle East:

> One sees this in the Islamisation of education. Every morning in Egypt they start with the reading of the Qur'ān; the texts of the teaching matter are full of references to Islam, whether in mathematics, in history or in literature; the learning of the Qur'ān is obligatory for all. Another instrument of this is the humiliation of the Christians at every level. If one walks along the street wearing – even discreetly – a cross, one risks being beaten or sworn at. It is common to be insulted by children ... At a more serious level, the economic one, the discrimination against Christians means that for them the possibility of finding work is more difficult, and frequently such a possibility is limited to working privately. In this respect one should not forget that most countries have an indication of the religion of the individual on the identity card, and even where this is not the case the name itself mostly reveals the religious faith of the individual and thus determines whether he will find work or how he will be treated....
>
> In the streets everywhere one hears the radio broadcasts with the five daily prayers, preceded by the call to prayer, which can last up to an hour. In Egypt it is the state radio which broadcasts the Qur'ān 24 hours a day ... The effect nonetheless is that anyone who is a Christian has to listen the whole day to the Qur'ān ...
>
> This combination of coercive forces is similar in many respects to what happened in the Communist countries, where the laws and the institutions guaranteed freedom in theory but in reality it was not so. When we recall that in 70 years communism almost succeeded in its attempts to extinguish the religious sense of the Russian people, then we must acknowledge that, if after so many centuries in the Middle East there are still Christian communities at all, then this is truly a miracle.[8]

---

[8]'Interview with Father Samir Khalil Samir' <http://www.alleanzacattolica.org/acs/acs_english/report_98/aaa_appendices.htm>, accessed Dec. 2006.

Writing on the treatment of the Coptic minority in Egypt, David Zeidan enumerates similar difficulties and many more. He concludes that official Islamic teaching has resulted in Muslims viewing religious minorities in their midst as traditional Muslim men view their women: inferior, segregated, weak, with specific limited functions in society, obliged to manifest modesty and humility in their behaviour, not equal before the law – yet protected by the stronger group and in a curious way bearing its honour. The Muslim male is bound to protect his womenfolk from any breach of honour; similarly Muslims are honour bound to protect 'their' *dhimmis* from attacks by outsiders.[9]

Sporadic communal violence against Christian minorities occurs in such countries as Egypt, Northern Nigeria, Pakistan and Indonesia. In some cases, local authorities have been complicit in this violence or quiescent in their response to it. Direct attacks on Christian minorities by radical Islamic groups have also taken place in countries like Algeria, Egypt, the Philippines, Indonesia, Turkey and Pakistan.[10] These attacks have increased in the last few decades with the rise of Islamic fundamentalism. Muslim radicals, in line with mainstream Muslim teaching, continue to use terms like kufr (unbelief) to refer to everything that is non-Islamic. They regard non-Muslims as 'infidels' who are 'enemies' of God. To such radicals, the only conceivable relationship between Muslims and non-Muslims involves jihad.

Other Voices and Perspectives

What I have set out above is the official, orthodox, mainstream teaching of Islam. These teachings remain on the statute books, so to speak, and have been enforced in varying degrees at various times in various places. This does not, however, mean that every Muslim knows these teaching, let alone believes and practises them. On the contrary, the vast majority of ordinary Muslims hardly know the teaching of Islam in detail. Many hardly even say their prayers consistently. Many educated Muslims adopt a more liberal and moderate understanding of Islam. In Muslim

---

[9] David Zeidan, 'The Copts: Equal, protected or persecuted? The impact of Islamization on Muslim–Christian relations in modern Egypt', in *Islam and Christian–Muslim Relations*, Vol. 10, No. 1 (1999): 57–61.
[10] See Paul Marshall, 'Present-day persecution of Christians', *Evangelical Review of Theology*, Vol. 24, No. 1 (2000): 27ff.

countries, those who call for strict observance of Islam hardly ever win elections (among the few exceptions are Algeria in the early nineties and Northern Nigeria in the late nineties). The majority of ordinary Muslims, especially Muslim women, are just as concerned about the strict teaching of Islam as non-Muslims. Moreover there are many sects and divisions with different interpretations of Islam.

The vast majority of Muslims living as minorities in sub-Saharan Africa, the West, India and other places want to live at peace and on equal terms with their non-Muslim relatives, friends and neighbours. Even though most may not necessarily disagree with the strict teaching of Islam, they know it is not in their interest to actively pursue its implementation. However, where Muslims are in the majority, as in North Africa, the Middle East and South-East Asia, the situation is quite different and non-Muslim minorities face discrimination and persecution.

The response of respected liberal Muslim intellectuals to the plight of these minorities is muted, to say the least. Most avoid the issue, others rationalise it, and some openly state that Muhammad's example in seventh-century Arabia should remain 'the standard Muslim treatment of Jews and Christians'.[11] There are also those who take a critical view of human rights in Islam and the condition of women in Islamic countries, but insist that these have nothing to do with true Islamic teaching and everything to do with culture. But such an argument is mere intellectual acrobatics. If the limitations and restrictions placed on women in Islamic societies arise solely from the culture of those societies, why is this culture so universal in Muslim societies from Asia through the Middle East to Africa? If these negative tendencies are the result of misunderstanding and misrepresentation of Islam, how is it that Islamic societies across geographical, cultural and racial boundaries have been wrong about these issues ever since the religion began in the seventh century? It would be much more realistic and credible to admit that these are part of Islamic teaching, but that they need to be reassessed in the light of contemporary realities.

A small but growing minority of Muslim intellectuals are genuinely seeking a critical rethinking or reformation of Islam in the light of our increasingly pluralistic and interdependent world. One such scholar is the Sudanese Abdullahi Ahmed An-Na'im, who states

---

[11] Fazlur Rahman, *Islam*: 28.

there is a fundamental tension, for example, between sharia notions of the Muslim umma (the exclusive community of Muslims) and national unity among Muslim and non-Muslim citizens of the modern nation state. At the international level, the sharia's legitimation of the use of force in jihad and direct action in furtherance of 'Islamic' objectives can hardly be reconciled with the modern principles of equal sovereignty of non-Muslim states and the rule of law in international relations.[12]

Similarly, former President Abdurrahman Wahid of Indonesia openly opposed the Islamic teaching regarding dhimmi and called for equal citizenship for all, regardless of their religious affiliations:

> My belief and the very core of my own existence reject *dhimmism* because, as an Indonesian and because of our national priorities, my main thinking is that I have to reject it. All citizens are equal. That is the problem. That is why I do not know what to do with it. It is there [in Islamic thought] but I reject it. So that means plurality should be there in the sense of let everybody live according to their own respective ways … So in the last analysis if I have to choose between the constitution and the concept of Islamic *Shari'ah* on this point I will follow the constitution.[13]

Like An-Na'im, Wahid acknowledges that this difficult teaching is enshrined in mainstream Islamic thought. But he rejects it because he deems it unhelpful in the Indonesian context. So does Asghar Ali Engineer, a leading Indian Muslim intellectual, who also propounds a reformist and progressive form of Islam.[14] Farid Esack, a leading South African Muslim intellectual, also honestly acknowledges the difficulties within Islamic teaching and calls for a more critical and radical reinterpretation of Qur'ānic teaching on non-Muslims.[15]

---

[12] Abdullahi Ahmed An-Na'im, 'Islam and Human Rights in Sahelian Africa', in D. Westerlund and E. E. Rosander (eds.), *African Islam and Islam in Africa*: 89.
[13] Abdurrahman Wahid, cited in Abdullah Saeed, 'Approaches to *Ijtihad* and neo-modernist Islam in Indonesia', in *Islam and Christian–Muslim Relations*, Vol. 8, No. 3 (1997): 291–92.
[14] Asghar Ali Engineer, *Rethinking Issues in Islam* (Mumbai: Orient Longman, 1998).
[15] See Farid Esack, *Qur'ān, Liberation and Pluralism: An Islamic Perspective of Interreligious Solidarity against Oppression* (Oxford: Oneworld Publications, 1997).

At present, these individuals and their perspectives remain on the fringes of mainstream Islam. In fact, some of those who propound such views have been executed, and most have been threatened with or endured physical attacks that have led to their seeking refuge in the West. But in the wake of 11 September 2001, a wind of serious soul-searching is blowing across the Muslim world. This wind seems to be blowing against the tide of conservative extremism and in favour of critical and progressive interpretations of Islam.

Our hope for a peaceful, pluralistic and interdependent world is going to be determined to a large extent by the outcome of this debate among Muslims rather than by multi-billion missile-defence systems or wistful thinking by politically correct Western academics and media. Some scholars have suggested that a faithful reading of the Qur'ān can only lead to the intolerant, triumphalistic and militant Medinan model of Islam.[16] If this is the case, Muslims are trapped in their traditions. But I am of the opinion that the Qur'ān is made for Muslims and not Muslims for the Qur'ān. Muslims therefore have the power, if they truly desire it and wish to be part of an interdependent pluralistic and democratic world order, to interpret the Qur'ān in terms that fit with contemporary realities. I fully agree with Thomas Friedman that

> What matters is not what Muslims tell us they stand for. What matters is what they tell themselves, in their own languages, and how they treat their own. Without a real war of ideas to sort that out – a war that progressives win – I fear we are drifting at best toward a wall between civilizations and at worst toward a real clash.[17]

But while this debate rages among Muslims, what is an appropriate Christian response? How should Christians witness to Islam? That will be the topic of chapter eleven, but before we go there, we need to understand how Muslims see Jesus, the central figure in Christianity.

---

[16] See Christian W. Troll, 'Sharing Islamically in the pluralistic nation-state of India: The views of some contemporary Indian Muslim leaders and thinkers' in *Christian–Muslim Encounters*, Y. Y. Haddad and W. Haddad (eds.) (Miami: University of Florida Press, 1995): 245–62. See also D. Marshall, *God, Muhammad and the Unbelievers: A Qur'anic Study* (London: Curzon Press, 1999): 196–97.

[17] Thomas L. Friedman, 'Islam and the Pope': 7.

10

Jesus in Islam

Jesus and his mother Mary are held in high esteem in Islamic sources.[1] It is even reported that when Muslims captured the Ka'bah in 630, Muhammad ordered that all the statues there should be destroyed except for those of Mary and Jesus. In fact, right from the beginning, Muhammad saw himself as the immediate successor of Jesus. A tradition reports him as saying, 'I am the nearest of mankind to Jesus son of Mary – on both of whom be peace – because there has been no Prophet between him and me'.

Why Study Jesus in Islam?

Some people might wonder why it is necessary to concern ourselves with what people of other faiths, and particularly Muslims, have to say about Jesus Christ. Kwame Bediako's response to this question is astute:

> Strange as it may seem, theological affirmations are meaningful ultimately, not in terms of what adherents say, but in terms of what persons of other faiths understand those affirmations to imply for them. In other words, our Christian affirmations are validated when their credentials and validity are tested not only in terms of the religious and spiritual universe in which Christians habitually operate, but also – indeed especially – in terms of the religious and spiritual worlds which persons of other faiths inhabit. For it is in those 'other worlds' that the true meaning of Jesus Christ becomes apparent and validated. Christian history shows that as Christian faith engages with new cultures, new insights about Jesus Christ emerge.[2]

---

[1] For more information on this topic, see John Azumah, 'Islamic Christology: A Case of Reverential Disavowal', in *Journal of African Christian Thought*, Vol. 8 No. 1, June 2005: 50–60

We are called not only to confess Jesus Christ as Lord and Saviour, but also to witness to this truth about him. Our witness, as Bediako points out, stands to be enriched by new insights that can be gained from other points of view. With this in mind, we shall seek to delineate some of the key theological agreements and disagreements between Islam and Christianity as regards the identity and mission of Jesus.

Jesus' Birth

Sixty-four of the 93 verses in the Qur'ān that speak about Jesus are found in the nativity narratives in Suras 3 and 19. Kenneth Cragg observes that if the Gospels are said to be really passion narratives with extended introductions, 'it could well be said that the Jesus cycle in the Qur'ān is nativity narrative with attenuated sequel'.[3] *Maryam*, or Mary the mother of Jesus, is greatly honoured in Islam. She is the only woman mentioned by name in the Qur'ān (34 times) and a whole chapter (19) is named after her. She is identified as the daughter of Imnran, the sister of Aaron (3:35; 19:28),[4] and is described as a chaste woman whom God chose, made pure and preferred to all the women of creation (3:42). Before her birth, her mother pledged her unborn child to God. She was greatly distressed when she gave birth to a girl, and asked that she and her daughter be protected from Satan. Mary was put under the guardianship of Zachariah in the temple, where she was miraculously fed.[5]

The Qur'ān contains two accounts of the annunciation of Jesus' coming birth (3:33–49; 19:16–34). In Sura 3, God is said to have sent an angel to Mary, while in Sura 19, it was a spirit that was sent to give her the good news. The angel appeared to Mary and addressed her in the following words:

> O Mary! Allah giveth thee glad tidings of a word from Him, whose name is the Messiah, Jesus, son of Mary, illustrious in

---

[2] Kwame Bediako, 'Christianity, Islam and the Kingdom of God: Rethinking their relationship from an African perspective', in *Journal of African Christian Thought*, Vol. 17, No. 2 (Dec. 2004): 6

[3] K. Cragg, *Jesus and the Muslim: An Exploration* (Oxford: Oneworld Publications, 1999): 19

[4] In Numbers 26:59, Amram is the father of Moses, Aaron and Miriam (or Maryam). This passage suggests that the Qur'ān is confusing Miriam, the sister of Moses, with Mary the mother of Jesus.

[5] The apocryphal *Protevangelium of James* contains the story of Mary being fed by angels in the temple.

the world and the Hereafter, and one of those brought near (unto Allah). He will speak unto mankind in his cradle and in his manhood, and he is of the righteous (3:45–46).

When Mary queried how this was going to be since no man had known her, the angel assured her that God could do anything. Some Muslim exegetes state that the angel then breathed into a slit in Mary's cloak, which she had taken off. When she put it on again, she conceived Jesus. However it was done, Mary conceived and withdrew to a distant place. When the time came, she gave birth under a palm tree and took the child home to her people. She was accused of having brought shame and dishonour to her family. In response, Mary simply pointed to the infant Jesus lying his cradle, who then spoke the following words:

> Lo! I am the slave of Allah. He hath given me the Scripture and hath appointed me a Prophet, And hath made me blessed wheresoever I may be, and hath enjoined upon me prayer and almsgiving so long as I remain alive, And (hath made me) dutiful toward her who bore me, and hath not made me arrogant, unblest. Peace on me the day I was born, and the day I die, and the day I shall be raised alive! (19:30–33).[6]

Jesus as Son of God

Although the Qur'ān accepts the virgin birth, the incarnation is strongly and repeatedly rejected. His miraculous birth is not considered to prove that he was either the Son of God or God. The Qur'ān strongly condemns the very idea and insists that Jesus is no more than a human being and a prophet:

> The Messiah, son of Mary, was no other than a messenger, messengers (the like of whom) had passed away before him. And his mother was a saintly woman. And they both used to eat (earthly) food! (5:75).

In arguing that Jesus is a created being, Muslims cite the angel's words to Mary when she asks how she can have a child while still a virgin. The

---

[6] The Arabic and Syrian versions of the *Infancy Gospels*, which are said to have been in circulation in Arabia during the time of Muhammad, also have Jesus speaking from the cradle to announce his identity and mission.

angel replies that when God wills something he commands it 'Be! and it is' (3:47). On the strength of this verse, Muslim theologians insist that Jesus was a creature made by God, the creator who has no associate.

Muslims also argue that the creation of Adam was even more marvellous than that of Jesus. God created Adam from dust and commanded him into being (3:59). He had no father and no mother, did not have to go through the normal developmental stages of life, and was honoured by God who asked his angels to prostrate themselves before him (i.e. worship him). If unusual birth makes one the Son of God or God, then, Muslims argue, Adam qualifies even more than Jesus!

Mainline Islamic teaching about Jesus is summed up in the following quotations from the Qur'ān:

> O People of the Scripture! Do not exaggerate in your religion nor utter aught concerning Allah save the truth. The Messiah, Jesus son of Mary, was only a messenger of Allah, and His word which He conveyed unto Mary, and a spirit from Him. So believe in Allah and His messengers, and say not 'Three'. Cease! (it is) better for you! Allah is only One God. Far is it removed from His transcendent majesty that he should have a son. His is all that is in the heavens and all that is in the earth. And Allah is sufficient as Defender (4:171).
>
> They surely disbelieve who say: Lo! Allah is the Messiah, son of Mary. The Messiah (himself) said: O Children of Israel, worship Allah, my Lord and your Lord. Lo! whoso ascribeth partners unto Allah, for him Allah hath forbidden Paradise. His abode is the Fire. For evildoers there will be no helpers. (5:72).

Indeed the Qur'ān reports Jesus denying ever instructing his disciples to take him and his mother as gods along with God (5:116).

The Qur'ānic denial that Jesus is the Son of God is based on the idea that his conception would have required God to physically take Mary as his wife. The term used for 'child' in all except one of the verses denying that God has offspring is *walad*, a word which denotes physical conception. The Qur'ān thus asks: 'How can He have a child, when there is for Him no consort?' (6:101). In other words, for Allah to have a child, he must take a spouse, and it is not in his nature to do such a thing. Yusuf Ali, one of the leading Qur'ānic commentators of the last century, sums up the Islamic position in the following words:

> Begetting a son is a physical act depending on the need of men's animal nature. God Most High is independent of all needs, and it is derogatory to Him to attribute such an act to Him. It is merely a relic of pagan and anthropomorphic superstitions. Such an attribution to God of a material nature, and of the lower animal functions of sex is derogatory to the dignity and glory of God. The belief in God begetting a son is not a question of words or of speculative thought. It is a stupendous blasphemy against God. It lowers God to the level of an animal.[7]

The Islamic position seems to have been influenced by the pre-Islamic Arab belief that God had daughters in the form of female deities whose intercession was sought. In fact the Qur'ānic denials of God having children were first directed at the pre-Islamic Arabs, who are accused of preferring sons for themselves, but assuming that God only has daughters (53:19–22). It appears that these denials were then extended to the Christian teaching about Jesus being the Son of God without a good understanding of what Christians mean by that title. Unfortunately, this position remains the orthodox Muslim teaching regardless of Christian protestations to the contrary.

Jesus as God

The Islamic denial of the deity of Jesus is rooted in core Qur'ānic teaching and Islamic beliefs about the Oneness of God (*tawhid*), his transcendence, and the nature of revelation.

The core message of the Qur'ān is that Allah is *wahid*, the sole divinity. The assertion 'Lo! thy Lord is surely One' (37:4) is at the very core of Muhammad's preaching concerning God, and is constantly repeated throughout the Qur'ān (e.g. 'It is inspired in me that your God is One God – 41:6; see also 2:163). Indeed, belief in the Oneness of God forms the cornerstone of the Islamic witness or Shahadah: 'I bear witness that there is no God but Allah, and that Muhammad is the Messenger of Allah.'

---

[7] See Christian Troll, 'Jesus Christ and Christianity in Abdullah Yusuf Ali's English interpretation of the Qur'ān', in *Islamochristiana*, Vol. 24 (1998): 93–94

Sura 112 of the Qur'ān is the sura of unity (tawhid) par excellence: it stresses that God Alone is the Master, not begetting and not begotten, without equal. It asserts the unity of the divine nature, whose intrinsic mystery cannot be fathomed (see also 23:91). God the creator is unique and totally other; to associate anything or anyone with him constitutes *shirk*, the greatest and unpardonable sin. Consequently the Christian teaching that God took human form and came to dwell with human beings is both alien and repugnant to Islam. God is absolute and transcendent – the very possibility of Emmanuel (God with us) is unthinkable. As long ago as the tenth century, a Muslim scholar in a correspondence with a Christian expressed this repugnance as follows:

> In your error, your ignorance and your presumption in the face of God – Praise and Glory to Him – you still pretend that God came down from His Majesty, His Sovereignty, His Almighty Power, His Light, His Glory, His Force, His Greatness and His Power, even to the point of entering into the womb of a woman in suffocating grief, imperfection, in narrow and dark confines and in pain, that he stayed in her during nine months to come out as do all the sons of Adam, that he was then fed at her breast during two years, behaved as any child does and grew as any other child, year by year, crying, sleeping, eating, drinking, experiencing hunger and thirst during the whole of his life. Well then: who was ruling the heavens and the earth? Who was holding them? Who made laws for them? Who dictated the course of the sun, the moon, the stars, of the night, of the day, and of the winds? Who created? Who gave life and death while Isa was in the womb of his mother and after he came into the world? Praise and Glory to God![8]

However, just as Christians have debated whether Jesus was divine or human, and have finally settled on the position that he is fully divine and fully human, so Muslims have debated the nature of the Qur'ān. As the literal word of God, is the Qur'ān created and therefore not eternal? Or is it uncreated and therefore eternal and divine? The official position, reached in the early tenth century, is that Muslims should believe in the Qur'ān as uncreated and eternal 'without asking how' (*Bila Kayf*).

---

[8] Umar's Letter to Leo, cited in Jean-Marie Gaudeul, *Encounters and Clashes: Islam and Christianity in History, Vol. II* (Rome: Pontificio Istituto di Studi Arabi e d'Islamistica, 2000): 153.

The role of Muhammad in the revelation of the Qur'ān is comparable to that of the Virgin Mary in Christianity. Just as God chose to reveal his Son through Mary in Christianity, so he chose to reveal his will through the 'illiterate' Muhammad.

It may be that the issue of the nature of revelation is an area in which Christians and Muslims can hope for constructive dialogue on Christological questions.

Jesus' Mission and Miracles

According to the Qur'ān, Jesus was no more than a prophet. His mission was primarily to the children of Israel, whereas Muhammad's mission was universal. Jesus was a sign from God for humanity, strengthened by the Holy Spirit (5:110, 2:87). He was taught Scripture by God (3:48).

The content of Jesus' teaching, for example, the Sermon on the Mount, is barely mentioned in the Qur'ān. All that is said is that he came to confirm the truth in the Torah and make lawful what was hitherto declared unlawful (3:50, 4:46, 3:93). He came to clarify previous revelations (43:63), enjoin the fear of the one God, and warn against ascribing partners to God (5:72). The religion Jesus established was the same as that of Noah, Abraham, Moses and subsequently Muhammad – or in other words, Islam (33:7, 42:13). The *injil* (gospel) given to Jesus contains guidance, light and admonition (5:46) as well as good tidings about the coming of an 'unlettered prophet' (7:157). The gospel and message preached by Jesus have, however, been tampered with and corrupted by successive generations of Christians. Jesus himself prophesied the coming of a prophet named *Ahmad* or 'the praised one' (61:6). The *Gospel of Barnabas*, which has been proved beyond any doubt to be a fictitious work produced in Spain in the late sixteenth and early seventeenth century, develops this theme more fully.[9] In this so-called 'gospel', Jesus predicts the coming of Muhammad by name, and Muhammad, rather than Jesus, is identified as the Messiah.

Jesus and Mary are the only two people whom the Qur'ān describes as sinless (3:36, 46). Islam rejects the concept of original sin, but

---

[9] Jan Slomp, 'The *Gospel of Barnabas* in recent research', in *Islamochristiana*, Vol. 23 (1997): 81–109. The Gospel of Barnabas clearly contradicts the Qur'ān by referring to Muhammad rather than Jesus as the Messiah. Strangely, it refers to Jesus as 'Christ' but reports him denying that he is the Messiah.

nevertheless there is a tradition which states that 'every son of Adam when newly born is touched (or probably squeezed) by Satan [and infected with sin] … it is at this contact that the child utters his first cry.'[10] The only exceptions were Mary and Jesus, both of whom were granted the extraordinary privilege of being preserved from any contact with the devil at the instant of their birth. They are unique, for the Qur'ān reports other prophets falling into temptation, sinning and asking for forgiveness – Adam (7:22–23), Abraham (26:82), Moses (28:16), Jonah (37:142) and Muhammad (3:31; 47:19).

Many traditions abound about Jesus' omniscience and supernatural powers both as a child and an adult. He is the only one, apart from God, with the power to create life (birds) by using clay and breathing life into them (3:49). This tradition about his modelling of birds is found in the apocryphal gospels (the *Gospel of Thomas*, chapter 2; the *Arabic Gospel of the Infancy* chapters 1, 36, 46; and the *Armenian Gospel of the Infancy* chapters 18 and 2). Christian apologists have always pointed out that the verb *khalaqa,* used of Jesus' creating birds, is a verb that the Qur'ān elsewhere uses exclusively to refer to God's activity. The substance used, clay, is what God used to create the first man, Adam (6:2; 7:12; 28:38). The act of breathing into the birds is similar to the way God breathed into Adam and into Mary. The breath of Jesus, like that of God, has the power to give life. This point should not be dismissed lightly.

The Qur'ān acknowledges that Jesus was the only one of all the prophets to be given the power to heal the sick and raise the dead, and says that he performed all these miracles by the permission of God (5:110). But it denies that these unique signs of healing and even giving of life indicate that Jesus is something more than a prophet. Muslims argue that other prophets, especially Moses, performed even greater miracles than Jesus did. Responding to Christian use of Jesus' miracles as signs of his divinity, a tenth century Muslim noted:

> And if you are to consider Isa as a god only because he raised the dead to life, cured the sick, and accomplished miracles with the permission of God, then (I would answer) that Hazqil [Ezekiel; Ezek 37] also raised the dead to life, as you can see in your book, thirty-five thousand people … many more than were raised by Isa and yet you have not made him into a god.

---

[10] G. C. Anawati, 'Isa', in *Encyclopaedia of Islam* CD-ROM edition.

In the same way Elyas [Elisha] raised to life the son of the old woman as you maintain ... The miracles of Isa are not superior to those accomplished by Musa in the presence of Pharaoh's magicians ... And both of them only did what they did with the permission of God, on His order, and in virtue of His Decree, because God decides in His wisdom, and acts with Power.[11]

On the whole, Muslim commentators regard Jesus' mission as a failure at worst and an unfinished or preparatory task at best. They point out that he never married, achieved military victory over his enemies, or attained temporal power. By contrast, Muhammad 'wrought a mighty revolution and made the Arabs master of the then civilized world' whereas Jesus 'could not free his people from the yoke of the Romans'.[12]

Jesus' teaching in the Sermon on the Mount is derided as impracticable, unrealistic and too docile. One Muslim writer describes it as 'pathetic and escapist', appeasing the Roman overlords by making virtue out of suffering and oppression and preventing action in this world by offering consolation in the next. He goes on to describe the Sermon on the Mount as 'meek and spineless'.[13] In other words, Jesus failed to achieve manifest success. But Muslims then have to face the problem of explaining how a prophet could be a failure. Does this represent a failure on God's part? In an apparent attempt to resolve this problem, Islam teaches that Jesus will return to earth before the end of the world to accomplish what he could not do in his earlier life. This second coming is known as the 'Descension of Jesus' – *nuzul 'Isa*. This belief is derived from Sura 43:61, which talks of Jesus being the 'sign of the hour'. Tradition has surrounded this rather oblique reference with a mass of detail. Some of these details are as follows: On returning to the earth, Jesus will descend onto the white arcade of the eastern gate at Damascus or (according to another tradition) onto a hill in the Holy Land. His head will be anointed. He will have in his hand a spear with which he will kill the Antichrist (*al-Dajjal*). Then he will go to Jerusalem at the time when the imam is leading the dawn prayer. The imam will try to

---

[11] Umar, cited in Jean-Marie Gaudeul, *Encounters and Clashes: Islam and Christianity in History, Vol II* (Rome: Pontificio Istituto di Studi Arabi e d'Islamistica, 2000): 154.
[12] See Kate Zebiri, *Muslims and Christians Face to Face* (Oxford: Oneworld Publications, 1997): 63–66.
[13] See Zebiri, *Muslims and Christians*. 63–66.

give up his place to him, but Jesus will put the imam in front of him and will pray behind him, as prescribed by Muhammad.

Then he will kill all pigs, break the cross, destroy synagogues and churches, and kill all Christians except those who believe in him (following 4:159). Once he has killed the false Messiah, all the Peoples of the Book (Jews and Christians) will believe in him, and there will be only one community (the Islamic umma). Jesus will make justice reign. Peace will be so complete that it will extend even to man's relations with the animals and to the relations among animals. Jesus will remain for forty years, will get married and have children, and will then die. The Muslims will arrange his funeral and will bury him at Medina, beside Muhammad.[14] To sum up, Jesus will complete the mission that had been cut short. As a prophet of God, he must not only succeed; he must also be seen to have succeeded.

Contemporary mainstream Muslim writers see the mission of Jesus principally as preserving the Torah and announcing the coming of Muhammad and regard Islam as a culmination and replacement of whatever he taught. S. H. Nasr, for instance, sees Muhammad as synthesising the elements of faith, law, and the spiritual way as represented by Abraham, Moses and Jesus respectively.[15] Cragg notes that

> If Jesus … supplies Islam with its eschatological perception and goal, Muhammad supplies the historical realism which is wanting in Jesus and precluded by his context. If Islamic traditions need to anticipate a Christ-style future, Jesus needed to anticipate a Muhammad-style future, the one in eternal the other in temporal terms. The Gospel may have it right in the ultimate; but the Qur'ān has it right in the concrete.[16]

In talking about the Qur'ānic view of Jesus and his mission, however, the Christian theologian Hans Küng rightly observes that 'the portrait of Jesus in the Qur'ān is all too one-sided, too monotone, and for the most part lacking in content'.[17]

---

[14] G. C. Anawati, 'Isa', in *Encyclopaedia of Islam.*

[15] S. H. Nasr, *Islamic Life and Thought* (London: George Allen & Unwin, 1981): 210

[16] K. Cragg, *Jesus and the Muslim*: 53

[17] Hans Küng, 'Christianity and world religions: The dialogue with Islam as one model', in *The Muslim World*, Vol. 77, No. 2 (April 1987): 89

Jesus' Names and Titles

Despite vigorous Qur'ānic and Muslim denials that Jesus is divine, the Qur'ān gives him a series of honourable titles, some of which strongly hint at divinity. The list below includes most of the names and titles given to Jesus in the Qur'ān:

- *Isa* is Jesus' personal name, derived from the Syriac version of the Hebrew Yeshua or Jesus. It is used twenty-five times in the Qur'ān.
- *Nabi Isa* (Prophet Jesus) is the way Muslims commonly refer to Jesus.
- *Nabi Allah* (Prophet of God) is used only once in the Qur'ān with reference to Jesus (19:30–31), even though he is always listed among the prophets.
- *Rasul Allah* (Apostle or Messenger of God) is used ten times (e.g. 5:75; 61:6). Jesus is one of if not *the* favoured or exalted apostle of God (2:253).
- *Isa Ibn Maryam* (Son of Mary) is used twenty-three times in the Qur'ān. This title, which occurs only once in the New Testament (Mark 6:3), appears five times in the *Arabic Gospel of the Infancy* and fifteen times in the Syriac version of the same gospel, indicating that early Arab and Syrian Christians referred to Jesus in this way.
- *Abdallah* (Servant or Slave of God) is used three times (4:172, 19:30, 43:59). It simply means a creature indebted to God.
- *Al-Masihu,* (the Messiah) is used eleven times in the Qur'ān exclusively for Jesus. In the account of the annunciation, we read that 'His name shall be the Messiah, Jesus, Son of Mary' (3:45). However, according to the Qur'ān, this title does not make him any different from other prophets for 'the Messiah, son of Mary, was no other than a messenger' (5:75).
- *Wajih* (outstanding) is the way Jesus is described in 3:45. This word comes from *wajh*, meaning face, and indicates being in the forefront, pre-eminent, or highly honoured.
- *Muqarrab* (drawn near) is also used in 3:45 to describe Jesus' relationship with God. Elsewhere, the same word is used to refer to those who are admitted to Paradise (83:21, 28, 56:88) and to angels (4:172).
- *Âya* (sign) is the title assigned to Jesus when Gabriel tells Mary of God's intentions: 'We are to make him a sign for mankind' (19:21). The word translated 'sign' can also be translated as 'miracle'. It later came to be used to refer to the individual verses in the Qur'ān,

each of which is considered a miraculous sign from God. Muslim commentators take the 'sign' to which Gabriel refers to be Jesus' miraculous conception. Jesus himself is also reported as saying, 'I came to you with a sign from your Lord; so fear God and obey me' (3:50). Here the 'sign' may be any of the miracles Jesus performed. In Sura 21:90, the use of 'sign' is even more embracing: 'We made her and her son a sign for the world.' One would expect this verse to be interpreted as a reference to the universal scope of Jesus' mission.

- *Rahma* (mercy) is another title assigned at the annunciation, when Gabriel explains that Jesus is to be 'a mercy from us' (19:21).
- *Blessed* is another word applied to Jesus at his birth, where he is said to have spoken from his cradle and announced that God has 'made me blessed wheresoever I may be' (19:31).
- *Ayat ul-Allah* (Sign, Revelation or Token from God to the world) is used to describe Jesus in 19:21; 23:50. Traditionally, Muslim commentators have taken it to mean that Jesus is the 'Sign of the Hour', and that his second coming and all that he will accomplish then will signal the end of the world.
- *Kalimatu Allah* (Word of God) is one of most striking titles of Jesus for Christians. The Qur'ān uses it when the angel tells Mary: 'Allah giveth thee glad tidings of a word from Him, whose name is the Messiah, Jesus, son of Mary (3:45). Classical Muslim commentators have interpreted this title in various ways. Some say that Jesus is the fulfilment of the creating word of God, uttered at the moment of his conception; others that he is the prophet announced in the word of God, received and preached by the earlier messengers; others that he is the word of God because he speaks on behalf of God and thus leads men in the right way; and still others that he is a word of God because he is, in his own person, 'good tidings'.
- *Ruh Allah* (Spirit of God) is another striking title used for Jesus alone in the Qur'ān: 'The Messiah, Jesus son of Mary, was only a messenger of Allah, and His word which He conveyed unto Mary, and a spirit from Him' (4:171).

While Christians may be tempted to interpret some of the names and titles in the preceding list as pointing to the divinity of Christ, Islamic orthodoxy has vehemently insisted that all of them are honorific and that their meaning should be taken at face value. But all human races, and especially Semitic and African people, attach deep significance to names and titles. This point is evident not only from the Bible, but also from the practice of several people-groups today. Names, surnames, nicknames and titles are bestowed upon people and places in order to express their significance or some special circumstance relating to them. For instance, names can tell us where someone comes from and, in African cultures, the circumstances under which that person was born. Titles tell us something about what a person has achieved. As an African, I think it requires more faith to take all the names and titles given to Jesus in the Qur'ān only at face value than it does to admit that there is something unique and special about him, even among prophets!

Jesus' Passion

The Qur'ānic witness to Jesus' passion is even more problematic than its witness to his birth. It appears to deny either the crucifixion or that Jesus was the one crucified:

> And because of their saying: We slew the Messiah Jesus son of Mary, Allah's messenger. They slew him not nor crucified, but it appeared so unto them; and lo! those who disagree concerning it are in doubt thereof; they have no knowledge thereof save pursuit of a conjecture; they slew him not for certain, But Allah took him up unto Himself. Allah was ever Mighty, wise (4:157–58)

The passage is part of an invective against the Jews, who were apparently boasting about having crucified Jesus. The Qur'ān insists that the Jews did not kill Jesus but that it only 'appeared so unto them'. This part of the verse has been the subject of intense speculation by various Muslim commentators. Almost all agree that a crucifixion did take place, but that Jesus was not the victim. So the questions that have been debated are, firstly, what is meant by 'it appeared so unto them' and secondly, who was the victim? A common Muslim interpretation is that a substitute made to look like Jesus was crucified in his place. This view has tantalising parallels to the ancient Gnostics' position that a substitute died in place of Jesus, or that only Jesus' body was crucified while the true Jesus within did not suffer.[18] Various Islamic traditions and commentaries suggest the following possibilities:

- God outwitted the Jews and deluded them by making all of Jesus' disciples look like him at the time of his arrest. One of these disciples was then arrested and crucified.
- Simon of Cyrene, one of Jesus' disciples, volunteered to take on his likeness and his place on the cross.
- Jesus bribed his way out of the cross by promising paradise to one of his disciples (Sergus) who took his place.
- God cast the likeness of Jesus on Judas, who was crucified as punishment for his treachery.
- God outwitted the Jews by taking Jesus to heaven. To conceal this ascension, the Jews seized an innocent man, crucified him on an isolated hill, and barred anyone from coming to the place until the features of the body had changed beyond recognition.
- Pilate ordered his soldiers to free Jesus Barabbas but they mistakenly set Jesus of Nazareth free, who then escaped and went to meet with his disciples.[19]

According to the so-called *Gospel of Barnabas*, Jesus was whisked away to heaven by four angels and his likeness was cast upon Judas, who was then arrested, crucified and buried by the disciples, under the impression that he was Jesus. Some of the disciples then stole the body and started to spread lies about a resurrection. Jesus pleaded with God in heaven to let him go back and console his mother and disciples and God granted him three days. He then returned under the protection of the same four angels, met his mother and disciples on the Mount of Olives and explained what had actually happened. He warned them to stop spreading lies about his death and resurrection, after which he was taken back up into heaven.[20]

But these Islamic denials of Jesus' death are complicated by the existence of other Qur'ānic verses that allude to his death. The infant Jesus is reported to have said, 'Peace on me the day I was born, and the day I die, and the day I shall be raised alive!' (19:33). Zechariah invokes the same blessing on John the Baptist in 19:15, implying a real death and resurrection in each case.

In 3:55 God says to Jesus, 'Lo! I am gathering (*mutawaffika*) thee and causing thee to ascend unto Me'. The verb *tawaffa* is associated

---

[18] J. M. Robinson (ed.), *The Nag Hammadi Library in English* (Leiden: E. J. Brill, 1977): 245, 332, 334.

[19] See Neal Robinson, *Christ in Islam and Christianity* (London: Macmillan, 1991).

[20] See excerpts in J. M. Gaudeul, *Encounters and Clashes, Vol. II*: 175–78.

with death in the other twenty-five uses of it in the Qur'ān, including in 4:157, where it is used to deny that the Jews had killed Jesus. On three occasions, this verb refers to Muhammad's death. In fact Muhammad, arguing against the divinity of Jesus in a discussion with Christians from Najran, is reported to have asked them: 'Do you not know that our Lord is living and does not die, and that Jesus passed away?'[21] In this tradition, Muhammad appears to accept that Jesus died, and in fact uses his death as an argument against Christian claims of Jesus' divinity.

Mainstream Islamic teaching has continued to maintain that all references to the death of Jesus in the Qur'ān are eschatological (that is, they refer to his death forty years after his second coming). However, some individual Muslim commentators and writers have acknowledged that 3:55 and 3:48 may refer to a real death of Jesus. Some have said that Jesus died for three hours before being raised, others that he was dead for seven hours. Ibn Kathir (died 1373) simply said, 'God caused him to die for three days, then resurrected him, then raised him.'[22]

Mahmoud Ayoub, a Lebanese Shia Muslim living in the United States, is of the opinion that Muslim commentators have not been able to convincingly disprove the crucifixion. On the contrary, they have made the matter even more complicated by introducing the substitution theory. The Qur'ān, according to Ayoub, is not denying the crucifixion as a historical event but rather its theological implications. Rather than speaking about a righteous man who was wronged, the Qur'ān is speaking about the Word of God who was sent to earth and who returned to God. The denial of the killing of Jesus is thus a denial of the power of men to vanquish and destroy the divine Word, which is forever victorious.[23] Another highly respected contemporary Egyptian Muslim scholar declares:

> The idea of a substitute for Christ is a very crude way of explaining the Qur'ānic text. They had a lot to explain to the masses. No cultured Muslim believes in this nowadays. The text is taken to mean that the Jews thought they had killed Christ but God raised him unto Himself in a way we can leave

---

[21] Alfred Guillaume, *The Life of Muhammad*: 272.
[22] See Robinson, *Christ in Islam and Christianity*: 120–22.
[23] Mahmoud M. Ayoub, 'Towards an Islamic Christology, II. The death of Jesus: Reality or delusion', in *The Muslim World*, Vol. 70, No. 2 (April 1980): 116–118

unexplained among the several mysteries which we have taken for granted on faith alone.[24]

The Ahmadiyya Movement (see chapter 6) claims that Jesus was crucified on the cross, taken down in a coma and nursed by his disciples in a cave. He is said to have recovered and escaped to India in search of the lost tribe of Israel. He lived in India for 120 years, died and lies buried in Kashmir. It appears that in order to claim the title Messiah for himself, Ghulam Ahmad (the founder of the movement) had to find a grave for Jesus. Even more important, he wanted to counter the Christian argument that Muhammad is dead and buried in Medina while Jesus is alive with God in heaven.

The stance of the Ahmadiyya Movement and much of the Muslim attitude to Jesus seem to be shaped more by Christian claims that Jesus is superior to Muhammad than by Qur'ānic teaching. At the heart of the Islamic puzzle about the passion of Christ are the contrasting prophetic experiences of Muhammad and Jesus. When the Meccans plotted to kill Muhammad, he escaped, leaving his cousin Ali in his bed to deceive his pursuers. He hid in a cave for three days and then slipped away to Medina. From there, he organised his followers, fought his enemies and finally captured Mecca. So crucial is the hijra in Islam that this event, rather than the birth or death of Muhammad, marks the beginning of the Islamic calendar. When Muslims compare his escape with Jesus' capture in Gethsemane, they see the vindication of Muhammad in his rescue from his enemies and, more importantly, in his victories over them in subsequent battles. The image of a suffering prophet is therefore difficult to reconcile with what Kenneth Cragg calls the 'manifest victory' or 'success' associated with the prophetic office in Islam. As one key Muslim writer put it

> in the Qur'ān, everything is aimed at convincing the Believer that he will experience victory over the forces of evil … Islam refuses to accept this tragic image of the Passion. Not simply because it has no place for the dogma of the Redemption, but because the Passion would imply in its eyes that God had failed.[25]

---

[24] Muhammad Kamil Husain, *City of Wrong* (trans. K. Cragg: Amsterdam: 1958): 222
[25] Ali Merad, 'Christ according to the Qur'ān', in *Encounter* (1980): 14ff

Islamic objections to the passion of Christ are also rooted in contrasting views of what constitutes the human problem and the solution required. According to Christian teaching, Jesus is not just a prophet but also a saviour who came to redeem humanity from the power of sin by offering the ultimate sacrifice on the cross. Thus the doctrine of salvation (soteriology) is intimately associated with Christ's suffering and death. On the other hand, in Islam the human problem is not sin but ignorance of the will of God. What is needed is therefore a prophet who will bring guidance rather than a saviour bringing redemption.

Kenneth Cragg summarises the Islamic objections to the passion of Christ as follows: 'It did not, historically; it need not redemptively; and it should not morally happen to Jesus.'[26] Historically it did not happen because the Qur'ān denies it! Redemptively, it need not happen because 'Islam holds man to be not in need of salvation' but of success, which can be obtained with the right guidance of the law. Morally, it should not, because everyone is responsible for their own sins. Why should a just God hold one person responsible for the sins of another? Moreover, if the redemption of humanity from the power of sin is what Jesus set out to achieve through his death on the cross, then he failed because he ended his ministry with only a 'few believers' and human beings continue to live under the power of sin. Muslims therefore regard Jesus' death on the cross (assuming that they admit that this did happen) as a pathetic misadventure unworthy of a prophet of God, let alone one believed to be God. As one eleventh-century Muslim apologist put it:

> [Jesus] gave his blood freely, according to what you say, desiring to save mankind from error, and only a small number believed in him. Yet people believed in other Prophets who did not go so far as this ... Moses, on whom be peace, did not die till a large number believed in him, a great multitude; nor did Muhammad – may God bless him and give him peace – die till a huge number believed in him, who thereby gained possession of the lands and conquered the horizons, and God made him victorious over every religion ... If Jesus, on whom be peace, knew the Unseen, why did he give his blood through a desire

---

[26] K. Cragg, *Jesus and the Muslim*: 178
[27] Al-Baji (1012–1081), in J. Gaudeul, *Encounters and Clashes, Vol. II*: 182–83

for that which was not accomplished, and from which he gained nothing?[27]

With regard to the person, mission and passion of Christ, in Islam faith and belief take precedence over empirical historical evidence. It is futile to try to convince Muslims that some aspects of Islamic Christology are mistaken because they are not in line with the biblical accounts or empirical evidence. Any such suggestion strikes at the heart of the integrity of the Islamic faith. Making this point, Seyyed Hossein Nasr notes that it is God who revealed the Islamic doctrine of Christ to Muslims. If certain verses of the Qur'ān like those of Surāt Maryam are incorrect, then by what criterion should Muslims accept the rest of the Qur'ān? If certain verses of the Qur'ān are rejected because of some extrinsic argument or in order to make friends with Christians or achieve world peace or get into the United Nations, or for any other worldly reason, however laudable, then the rest of the Qur'ān must also be rejected as the Word of God.[28] Nasr explains further that 'even if [the crucifixion] had been recorded on film and thoroughly documented (God forbid), nevertheless the Islamic position would not *logically* [his emphasis] be destroyed.'[29] The point Nasr is making on behalf of all Muslims is that since the Muslim teaching about Christ is revealed by God and recorded in the Qur'ān, it cannot be contested let alone contradicted. The Qur'ān says Jesus was not crucified and no amount of 'evidence' can contradict that, since that would amount to questioning the integrity of God and the Qur'ān.

Jesus in Muslim Traditions and Devotion

While firmly rejecting the divinity of Jesus, Muslim traditions and devotion seem to have gone far beyond the usual interpretation of the Qur'ān in providing detailed accounts of Jesus' birth, physical features and ministry.

Islamic traditions tell that Mary conceived Jesus at the age of thirteen (others say fifteen). She and her cousin Joseph the carpenter lived and worked in a mosque as water-carriers. One day, Mary went to fetch

[28] Seyyed Hossein Nasr, 'Response to Hans Küng's Paper on Christian–Muslim Dialogue' in *The Muslim World*, Vol. 77, No. 2 (April 1987): 100
[29] S. H. Nasr's comments during discussions on 'Christianity and World Religions', in *The Muslim World*, Vol. 77, No. 2 (April 1987): 124

water and God sent Gabriel to her and made him resemble a 'handsome young man'.[30] And he said to her, 'O Mary, truly God hath sent me to you that I may give you a pious child.' When Mary said, 'I take refuge from you,' he said to her, 'Verily I am the apostle of thy Lord to give you a pious child.' She said, 'Shall there be to me a child, and no one has touched me, and I have committed no folly?' He said, 'That is true, but thy Lord finds a miracle easy.' And he breathed in the opening of her dress which she had taken off; and when he departed from her, Mary put it on, and so she conceived Jesus.

Joseph and Mary escaped to Egypt because Herod wanted to kill Jesus. While there, he was sent to school but was too clever to be taught by any teacher. He and his mother lived in the house of the ruler of Egypt and he performed one of his first miracles during the wedding ceremony of the king's son:

> The King made a feast and collected all the people of Egypt and fed them for two months. And when it was finished, certain people from Syria came to see him, and he did not know of their coming until they came down upon him. And on that day he had no drink for them. And when Jesus saw his anxiety on this account, He entered some of the chambers of the ruler in which there were rows of jars, and He passed by them one by one, touching them with His hand; and every time He touched one it was filled with drink until He came to the last one. And He was at that time twelve years old.

Unlike the Qur'ān, which gives no details about Jesus' healings and other miracles, Islamic traditions contain many colourful accounts of dazzling miracles. For example, when Jesus was describing Noah's ark to his disciples, they are said to have responded:

> 'If you had sent us some one who had seen the ark and could describe it to us, we would believe.' So He arose and came to a little hill, and struck it with His hand and took a handful of the earth and said, 'This is the grave of Shem, the son of

---

[30] Unless otherwise stated, all quotations in this section are taken from Samuel M. Zwemer, *The Moslem Christ: An Essay on the Life, Character and Teachings of Jesus Christ According to the Koran and Orthodox Traditions* (New York: American Trust Society, 1912), as found in the CD-ROM, *The World of Islam: Resources for Understanding Islam* (Colorado Springs: Global Mapping International/Fuller Theological Seminary, 2000).

Noah. If you wish, I will raise him for you.' They said, 'Yes;' and He called upon God by His greatest name, and struck the hill with His staff and said, 'Come to life by permission of God.' Then Shem, the son of Noah, came forth from his grave, white haired. And he said, 'Is this the resurrection day?' Jesus said, 'No, but I have called you out in the name of God Most High.' Shem had lived five hundred years and he was still young. So he told them the news of the ark. Then Jesus said to him, 'Die;' and he said, 'Only on one condition, that God protects me from the agonies of death.' Jesus granted his request by permission of God.

Another tradition, recounted by Said Kaab, describes Jesus as

a ruddy man, inclining towards white. His hair was not lank, and He never oiled it. He went barefooted; and He never owned a place, or a change of garments, or property or vesture or provisions, except His daily bread. And whenever the sun began to set, He would kneel and pray until the morning. He was in the habit of healing the sick and the lepers, and raising the dead by the will of God. He could tell those about Him what they ate in their houses, and what they laid up against the morrow. He walked on the face of the water on the sea. He had dishevelled hair, and His face was small. He was an ascetic in this world and greatly desirous of the world to come; diligent in serving God. And He was a wanderer in the earth till the Jews sought Him and desired to kill Him. Then God lifted Him up to heaven, and God knows best.[31]

Many Islamic traditions speak highly of Jesus' teaching and portray him not only as a modest self-effacing ascetic but as someone unique and special even amongst prophets. One of the most respected Muslim mystics, Al-Ghazali (died 1111) reports a tradition that when Jesus was asked 'Are there any on earth like you?', he answered: 'Whoever has prayer for his speech, meditation for his silence and tears for his vision, he is like me.'[32] One of the earliest and most famous sufis, al-Hallaj (died 922), while not speculating about the person of Jesus, was enthralled

---

[31] See S. M. Zwemer, *The Moslem Christ*: 56ff
[32] Cited in K. Cragg, *Jesus and the Muslim*: 49

by the mystery of the cross. His guiding ideal was union with God through an all-absorbing love, a love which could not find expression in enjoyment but only in suffering and the cross. A line from one of his poems reads: 'I will die in the religion of the cross. I need go no more to Mecca or Medina.' And so he died, crucified as a heretic.

Ibn-Arabi (died 1240), another celebrated Muslim mystic, also speculated about Jesus. He is responsible for popularising the title 'the seal of saints' (*khâtam al-anbiyâ'*) for Jesus, which corresponds to Muhammad's title 'the seal of prophets' (33:40). He argued that Muhammad brought definitive legislative prophecy; Jesus will bring definitive holiness when he returns, sealing all holiness from Adam to the end of time.

Merad Ali, a French Muslim of Algerian origin, is of the view that the classical commentaries 'do not shed light on the figure of Christ in the way he deserves'. He points out that 'everything in the Qur'ān points to the fact that Christ is seen as an exceptional event in the history of the world, an event pregnant with exceptional meanings'. Merad stresses the aura of mystery surrounding the person of Jesus in the Qur'ān; the use of terminology such as 'Spirit' and 'Word' when referring to him, terms which are used of no one else; and the uniqueness of the miracles attributed to him, in particular those of creation and healing. He accepts that the Qur'ān denies Christ's divinity, but finds it significant that 'at no time is the term *bashar* (human being) applied to Christ'. Merad ends on an open note, saying that the Qur'ān aims 'to provoke reflection rather than to furnish final answers'.[33]

Coming home to Africa, Amadou Hampâté Bâ (1900–1991), a Malian Muslim mystic and scholar, talks about what he calls 'the mysterious link which appears between the Qur'ānic name of Jesus and the name by which God has named himself'. Bâ uses numerology to calculate the numerical value of the name Allah and the title 'Messiah, son of Mary', exclusively given to Jesus in the Qur'ān. He concludes:

> Whoever is enlightened by this secret stops being amazed when he hears that Jesus participates, in a certain way, in the Essence of the Divine Being. Are not the Word and the Spirit of a being inevitably a part of him? But, the two expressions 'God's Word' and 'the Spirit of God' were attributed to the

---

[33] Merad Ali, 'Christ According to the Qur'ān', in *Encounters*, Vol. 69 (1980): 2–17

Virgin Mary's son by the Qur'ān itself ... I could, without trouble, without prejudice or fear, set myself to listen to the Christian Path and to appreciate, for example, the depth of the Gospel according to John, notably in the first three verses of its prologue: 'In the beginning was the Word, the Word was with God, the Word was God. He was in the beginning with God. All things came to be through him, without him nothing came to be'.[34]

Before a wrong impression is created that the Muslims mentioned above are Christians in all but name, it has to be said that whatever is said of Jesus in Muslim traditions and devotion, much more is said of Muhammad. The superiority of Muhammad is maintained in every way (see chapter three). In summarising the whole of Islamic Christology, Cragg notes:

> Islam has a great tenderness for Jesus, yet a sharp dissociation from his Christian dimensions. Jesus is the theme at once of acknowledgment and disavowal. Islam finds his nativity miraculous but his Incarnation impossible. His teaching entails suffering, but the one is not perfected in the other. He is highly exalted, but by rescue rather than by victory. He is vindicated, but not by resurrection. His servanthood is understood to disclaim the sonship which is its secret ... Islam has for him a recognition moving within a non-recognition, a rejectionism on behalf of a deep and reverent esteem.[35]

But what significance does Islamic Christology have for Christian witness? What are its implications for Christian witness? And in the light of these reflections, how are we to approach Islam and Christian witness to Muslims in the twenty-first century? These are the questions we will try to address in the next chapter.

---

[34] Cited from J. Gaudeul, *Encounters and Clashes, Vol. II*: 158–9

[35] K. Cragg, *Jesus and the Muslim*: 278–79

11

A Christian Response to Islam

The question likely to be asked after reading all that has been said about Islamic teaching is. 'How should Christians respond to Islam?' It is important to stress that any Christian response or witness has to be biblically based and Christ-like. In other words, our response or witness has to be guided by the question, 'What would Christ have done under such circumstances?' With this in mind, I will look at the responses from two perspectives: first that of Christians living outside the Muslim world, and then that of Christian minorities living in Muslim majority situations.

Christians in the Non-Muslim World

Christians living in the non-Muslim world like the West, most of sub-Saharan Africa and India need to get informed about the conditions endured by Christians in areas where Muslims are in the majority. Sadly, many Christians are completely oblivious to the plight of these Christian minorities.[1] Occasionally we hear or read about their suffering in the media and are momentarily horrified, but that is all. Very few Christians actually take it upon themselves to continually pray for these minorities.

In my view, the minimum that Christians in the non-Muslim world can do to help Christian minorities going through various forms of persecution is to stand in solidarity with them in prayer. Many Christians facing persecution in Muslim majority situations have come

---

[1] See a paper on "The Persecuted Church" in David Claydon, (ed.), *A New Vision, A New Heart, A New Call, Vol. One*, Lausanne Occasional Papers from the 2004 Forum for World Evangelization hosted by the Lausanne Committee for World Evangelization in Pattaya, Thailand, September 29 – October 5, 2004, (Pasedena: William Carey Library, 2005): 117-209. Also found in www.lausanne.org

to the conclusion that no one cares about them. Paul reminds us that as Christians, we are members of the body of Christ and the different parts of the body are arranged in such a way 'that there may be no discord in the body, but that the members may have the same care for one another. If one member suffers, all suffer together; if one member is honoured, all rejoice together' (1 Cor 12:25–26). In order to highlight the persecution of such Christians and bring their plight to the attention of the world, some Christians resort to extreme and desperate measures. One clear example of this is John Joseph, the Catholic bishop of Faisalabad, who committed suicide in a church on 6 May 1998 in order to draw attention to the situation of Christians in Pakistan.

But prayer alone is not enough! We must also act as advocates for the rights of all persecuted minorities, including Christian minorities in Islamic countries. Many Christians in the West and other parts of the non-Muslim world find very good excuses for why they cannot speak out against the persecution of Christians in Muslim countries. But if we look to Christ as our model, we see that he was a man who always stood by the weak, excluded and oppressed. In fact that was the core of his whole mission, as he declared at the very beginning of his ministry:

> The Spirit of the Lord is upon me, because he has anointed me
> to preach good news to the poor. He has sent me to proclaim
> release to the captives and recovering of sight to the blind, to
> set at liberty those who are oppressed (Luke 4:18).[2]

Despite all the protests and accusation that will follow any advocacy on behalf of minorities in Islamic countries, Muslim governments are very sensitive about the image of their regimes in the international community.

To give more credibility to our advocacy, Christians should try to link up with local Muslims who are equally appalled at the conditions endured by religious minorities in their communities. They will be more than willing to be partners in any struggle against all forms of discrimination, exclusion and persecution committed in the name of Islam. The famous words attributed to Martin Niemöller during the Holocaust in Nazi Germany should motivate all well-meaning people to

---

[2] All quotations from the Bible are taken from the *Revised Standard Version*, as contained in *BibleWorks* CD-ROM version 4.0.035p, (Norfolk, VA; BibleWorks, 1998).

stand in solidarity with oppressed minorities, irrespective of their creed or theological leanings:

> *First they came for the communists*
> *And I did not speak out –*
> *Because I was not a communist.*
> *Then they came for the socialists*
> *And I did not speak out –*
> *Because I was not a socialist.*
> *Then they came for the trade unionists*
> *And I did not speak out –*
> *Because I was not a trade unionist.*
> *Then they came for the Jews*
> *And I did not speak out –*
> *Because I was not a Jew.*
> *Then they came for me –*
> *And there was no one left*
> *To speak out for me.*[3]

Christians in the Muslim World

Christian minorities within Muslim majorities must guard against the tendency to pay back in kind, speaking the language the other party is supposed to understand best. Unfortunately, this is becoming common among many Christians in Muslim majority areas in sub-Saharan Africa, especially Nigeria and Sudan. There are countless instances of Christians in these and other situations taking revenge by resorting to violence and murdering Muslims. In West Africa, some Christians are even rejecting Jesus' pacificist teaching and adopting what they call 'third cheek theology'. Jesus said, 'If any one strikes you on the right cheek, turn to him the other also' (Matt 5:39). But many evangelical and charismatic Nigerian Christians are beginning to argue that they have now been struck several times on both cheeks, and no longer have a third cheek to turn!

There is no denying that many of these Christians have suffered untold persecutions at the hands of their Muslim neighbours and overlords.

---

[3] Martin Niemöller cited by Geneviève Jacques in *Beyond Impunity: An Ecumenical Approach to Truth, Justice and Reconciliation* (Geneva: WCC Publication, 2000): 10–11.

One has to be careful, therefore, not to be perceived as standing in judgement on their reactions in such situations. At the same time, one cannot help but point to Christians' fundamental calling, which is to be light and salt in a dark and tasteless world. To be light and salt is to make a difference. But in order to make a difference, one has to be different. Jesus made this point in Matthew 5:43–46:

> You have heard that it was said, 'You shall love your neighbour and hate your enemy'. But I say to you, Love your enemies and pray for those who persecute you, so that you may be sons of your Father who is in heaven; for he makes his sun rise on the evil and on the good, and sends rain on the just and on the unjust. For if you love those who love you, what reward have you? Do not even the tax collectors do the same?

A Sudanese bishop who felt he was being preached at by people who hardly believed his plight, let alone sympathised with him in it, once asked, 'How can I kiss the hand that has my head submerged under water?' Humanly speaking, Christ's command may sound impossible, but that is the witness we as Christians are called upon to make. When we resort to speaking the language of the persecutor, we not only damage our own witness but, in effect, join them in bearing their witness. Furthermore, acts of revenge carried out by Christians are clear signs of unbelief and lack of trust in the God we profess. For Paul admonishes, 'never avenge yourselves, but leave it to the wrath of God; for it is written, "vengeance is mine, I will repay, says the Lord"' (Rom 12:19). It is very difficult to say and even harder to carry to its logical conclusion, but history is full of examples of the fact that the church of Jesus Christ is built upon and thrives on the blood of martyrs.

I have always wondered about the helpfulness, even appropriateness, of the focus on post-Constantine Christianity in Protestant theological seminaries. When we talk about the history, mission and theology of the church, the first three centuries of Christianity are almost always glossed over. Students therefore leave seminaries with very little knowledge about this period. But if we are to equip the church for witness as a minority in difficult situations, the history, witness and theology of the early church need to be taught. It was through its faithful witness and perseverance through three centuries of persecution that the church was able to overcome the Roman Empire, the most powerful political entity the world has ever seen. How the early Christians achieved this feat despite being minorities in extremely difficult situations and the theology they drew upon are an inspiration and a model for Christians in similar situations today.

Christian Reflections on Islamic Christology

The main difficulty Christians may have with Islamic Christology is that

> Islamic convictions about Jesus and the Cross have never simply been those of mere investigators dealing with evidence. They have been those of believers persuaded already by theology.[4]

Islamic Christology is deeply rooted in the desire to safeguarding the *kalima* (the Islamic confession of faith): 'There is no god but God and Muhammad is the Prophet of God.' The unity and majesty of God, as well as the finality and superiority of Muhammad and Islam, remain the determining factors in Islamic Christology. The insistence that Jesus is not the Son of God is meant to safeguard the honour of God and keep Jesus and his mission in line with and in subservience to Muhammad, the Seal of the Prophets, and his 'final' and 'perfect' dispensation. Islamic Christology is therefore driven by the repeated Qur'ānic insistence that God has no partners and that Jesus is not the Son of God, rather than by what Christian Scriptures teach or what Christians actually believe. In this approach, Qur'ānic affirmations are taken at face value and 'evidence' is sought and conceived to confirm them. Moreover, while Islamic orthodoxy is busy Islamising Jesus, Muslim traditions and devotion are busy Christianising Muhammad.

Islamic Christology raises more questions than answers. For instance, God in Islam is all-powerful and almighty, capable of doing or wishing anything, yet he cannot have a son without having a wife? This is surely a serious limitation and an arbitrary restriction on the almighty and all-powerful God who has servants, slaves and messengers. Regarding the passion of Christ, it is worth noting that many verses in the Qur'ān insist that suffering was the lot of previous prophets, some of whom were even killed. It also insists that prophets, including Muhammad, are

---

[4] K. Cragg, *Jesus and the Muslim*:178.

mere mortals (3:138–9, 144–5) and that Jesus was no different (5:75). Yet the Qur'ān is reluctant to accept the death of Jesus, and may even completely deny it. What is so special about Jesus that his death, like his birth, is shrouded in mystery even in the Qur'ān? Surely, the two distinctive events of every mortal life are birth and death?

Jesus' virgin birth may be compared with the creation of Adam, while some of his miracles and titles may have been performed and shared by others. The same may be said of his 'rapture' to heaven. What remains indisputable, however, is that history has yet to produce any other human individual who combines all the elements in the picture painted of Jesus in the Qur'ān – someone who has a miraculous birth; who is sinless; who has the power to heal, raise the dead and create life; who experiences a miraculous rescue from death and who is then taken to heaven. Mainstream Christianity, grappling with the enigma of Jesus' identity, came to the conclusion that he is fully Man and fully God. Mainstream Islamic teaching, by contrast, both denies him divinity and fails to accord him full humanity. Far from providing a solution to the Jesus enigma, both Islamic and Christian theologies seem to have come up with their own puzzles.

One thing that is clear from the foregoing is that Muslims and Christians have driven themselves into a theological cul de sac. Christians insist that Jesus is the Son of God and indeed God himself; Muslims respond that God has no son and Jesus is only a prophet. Such doctrinal posturing does not lead to any meaningful dialogue.

Christians have to rethink Christology if it is to move from being a mere confession of faith to being a witness to the whole world and to Muslims in particular. It may be necessary, indeed vital, that we focus on the ministry of Jesus as well as on what it means for him to be the Son of God. Jesus' identity goes hand in hand with his mission and ministry. Reflecting on Colossians 2:15, Kwame Bediako notes that

> Biblical teaching clearly shows that Jesus is who he is (i.e. Saviour) because of what he has done and can do (i.e. save), and also that he was able to do what he did on the Cross because of who he is (God the Son).[5]

---

[5] K. Bediako, *Jesus in African Culture: A Ghanaian Perspective* (Accra: Asempa Publishers, 1990): 10.

Over the years, Christian theology has tended to present Jesus as if he is a set of ideas to be rationally argued and proven, rather than a person. This approach obscures his ministry and his relationship with ordinary people.

Muslim theologians, zealous for orthodoxy and anxious to protect the faithful from the influence of Christian neighbours, have also attempted to disprove Jesus as if he is a set of ideas. Yet despite the efforts of theologians and polemicists over the centuries, and the negative and even hostile literature about Jesus that they have produced, many Muslims around the world continue to be fascinated by Jesus. In a survey of over six hundred Muslim converts to Christianity from various parts of the world, one in four speaks of the role the figure of Jesus played in their religious development. Many speak of his appearing to them in dreams and visions, and sometimes in direct encounters. Their ideas may not be quite clear, but what is clear is that Jesus is encountered as a very real person: a master, a friend, someone who listens and helps. This Jesus is alive and draws people to himself just as he did the disciples who followed him, loved him and only slowly came to an awareness of his mysterious identity.[6] Christians should testify to this living Christ rather than engaging in fruitless debates about who he is and who he is not.

In witnessing, Christians should endeavour to present the person of Jesus and his relationship with various categories of people rather than arguing about his identity. Jesus is a provider for the poor and needy, a healer for the sick, a loving father for children and the fatherless, a helper of widows, a friend of the friendless and the untouchable, a rescuer of marginalised and despised people, and a champion opposing religious hypocrites and rich exploiters.

Jesus himself told Peter that flesh and blood cannot conceive of his true identity (Matt 16:17). It has to be revealed to people by God. Church history clearly teaches us that focusing on the identity of Jesus has caused irreparable pain and division in Christendom. It is a scar on the conscience of the church that the humanity, compassion, love and tolerance that Jesus lived, preached and died for were lost during the debates of the great church councils and at the time of the Inquisition. It is therefore crucial that in our dialogue with Muslims we do not

---

[6] See J. M. Gaudeul, *Called from Islam to Christ*: 313ff.

allow theoretical discussions and debates over his mysterious identity to distract us from the core of his mission.

In talking about Jesus being the Son of God, past and present Christian apologists and polemicists have always sought to draw comparisons between Jesus who is divine and Muhammad who is a mere mortal. These comparisons which seek to demonstrate the superiority of Jesus sometimes seem to miss the point. The Incarnation is, more than anything else, a humbling, self-emptying move on the part of God. Paul captures this fully in Philippians 2:5–10:

> Have this mind among yourselves, which you have in Christ Jesus, who, though he was in the form of God, did not count equality with God a thing to be grasped, but emptied himself, taking the form of a servant, being born in the likeness of men. And being found in human form he humbled himself and became obedient unto death, even death on a cross. Therefore God has highly exalted him and bestowed on him the name which is above every name, that at the name of Jesus every knee should bow, in heaven and on earth and under the earth …

Paul is reminding us that the one on whose behalf we make the claims 'did not count equality with God a thing to be grasped'; he is advising Christians to take on Christ's humility. Jesus preferred the form of a servant in order that he might carry out his mission of reconciling human beings to God. When the focus is on the superiority of Jesus, one sometimes wonders whose interest, or rather ego, is at stake – Christ's or our own.

Similarly, most Christians tend to refer to the miracles of Jesus as proof not only of his power but also of his superiority over others. The miracles speak for themselves, but the point most often missed is that Jesus did not perform them to demonstrate his power, nor did he go about trumpeting them. He performed miracles to meet specific needs and usually warned people not to talk about them. Indeed, on some occasions, whether with Satan in the temptation narrative or with people asking him to thrill them with miracles, he refused to yield to the temptation to be a 'miracle worker'.

Thus whether we are talking about Jesus being the Son of God, or about his virgin birth, the miracles he performed, his resurrection or his ascension, what is required of us as Christians is to resist the temptation to see these as ends in themselves. We are rather to endeavour to focus on their significance and necessity for our human existence and salvation. For instance, Jesus did not come as the Son of God in order to show his superiority over others but to radically redefine God's relationship with humanity. Through him, human beings can now relate to God as their Father. Through Jesus, God ceases to be a distant, unknown and unknowable ruler or master waiting to judge his miserable slaves and subjects; rather he is a loving father who is eager to forgive and accept us as his children. This transformation of status from that of slaves to that of children is particularly significant for Africans given their history of slavery at the hands of Muslim and Christian co-religionists from the East and West respectively. This is the witness that needs to occupy a central place in our African Christology as we engage with Muslims.

A Christian Theological Response to the Shari'ah

Seyyed Hossein Nasr, a leading Muslim intellectual, expresses Muslims' frustration with Christians who refuse to sympathise with, and indeed openly oppose, the introduction of the Islamic legal code, the Shari'ah.

> In Muslim-Christian debates, the Muslims have shared with Christians in their lack of comprehension of the view of the other side concerning law, but most of the pressure has come from the Christian side. Few Christians sympathise with Muslims who wish to return to the laws of their religion which were forcibly changed during the colonial period, while in general Muslims have been more sympathetic to Christians who wish to continue to live according to their traditional moral laws in a hedonistic society. Strangely enough, such Christians, many of whom are Evangelicals and born-again Christians, are those most opposed to Islam and the attempt of Muslims to live according to their religious laws as do such Christians themselves.[7]

Why should religious people, especially committed and practising ones such as evangelical Christians, oppose the introduction of God's law in

---

[7] Seyyed Hossein Nasr, 'Islamic–Christian dialogue: Problems and obstacles to be pondered and overcome', *Islam and Christian–Muslim Relations*, Vol. 11, No. 2 (July 2000): 217.

an increasingly irreligious (if not anti-religious) world? Muslims find this attitude very strange! Critics of the Shari'ah may argue that it is an outdated and barbaric system that belongs to seventh-century Arabia but, as Nasr points out, Shari'ah 'is no more outdated because it belongs to seventh-century Arabia, than the Sermon on the Mount would be outdated because it was pronounced 2000 years ago in Palestine'.[8]

Christians, and especially evangelicals, share Muslims' concern to accomplish God's will on earth. But evangelicals and many other African Christians still have difficulty with the option Muslims are proposing: the Shari'ah. Much has been said in preceding chapters about the historical and current difficulties Christians have with the Shari'ah. It is clear, however, that Muslims are not impressed by arguments that appeal to human rights. The quotation from Nasr implies that Muslims are expecting Christians to give religious or theological reasons for their opposition to the Shari'ah. That is what I will attempt to do in this section of the book.

As pointed out in earlier chapters, Islam teaches that a transcendent God does not, in fact cannot, reveal himself; God only reveals his will. Al-Faruqi sketches the difference between Islam and Christianity on this point in the following words:

> Christians talk about the revelation of God Himself – by God of God – but that is the great difference between Christianity and Islam. God is transcendent, and once you talk about self-revelation you have heirophancy and immanence, and then the transcendence of God is compromised. You may not have complete transcendence and self-revelation at the same time.[9]

The status of the Shari'ah as divine law in Islam derives from this belief that God reveals his will, and that this will is perfectly preserved in the Qur'ān and lived out by Muhammad. Hence the Qur'ān and Sunna form the principal sources of Islamic law.

Christians, too, actively seek the accomplishment of God's will on earth. They believe that something about God's will can be ascertained from the Bible and supremely in Jesus' life and works as recorded in the New Testament. But they believe that the will or mind of God remains

---

[8] Nasr, 'Islamic–Christian dialogue': 217.
[9] Isma'il Al-Faruqi, 'The nature of Islamic da'wah', in *Christian Mission and Islamic Da'wah: Proceedings of the Chambésy Dialogue Consultation* (Leicester: The Islamic Foundation, 1982): 48.

inexhaustible and unfathomable, beyond human comprehension. As God reminded the prophet Isaiah,

> my thoughts are not your thoughts, neither are your ways my ways … For as the heavens are higher than the earth, so are my ways higher than your ways and my thoughts than your thoughts (Isa 55:8–9).

Christians find it presumptuous to claim that any book offers full knowledge of the will or mind of God, especially if God is completely transcendent, as Islam teaches. It is at best risky and at worst dangerous for anyone to claim full knowledge of the mind or will of an unknown and, in fact, unknowable entity. Indeed, it is difficult to claim full knowledge of the mind or will of our fellow humans, or even of our very close relations and associates.

Thus to the Christian, the Muslim's belief that the Qur'ān contains the complete and perfect revelation of God's will sounds improbable. In the same way, to the Muslim, the Christian's belief that God has revealed himself fully in the person of Jesus Christ sounds implausible. These fundamental differences between Islam and Christianity have to be acknowledged and respected.

Related to this concern is the role Islam accords to prophets in general and to Muhammad in particular. Both Christians and Muslims believe in prophets and the role they play in communicating revelation. Like Muslims, Christians hold them in high regard and even revere them, but we view them as mere mortals and fallible beings who also stand in need of God's mercy and forgiveness. Though Christians respect Muhammad as the prophet of Islam, they have difficulty with the status given to his actions (recorded in the Sunna), which are regarded, along with the Qur'ān, as divine law for all time and places. Muhammad is coupled with God in certain key expressions of Muslim belief. The passages of the Qur'ān that were produced in Mecca insist on the ontological difference between Muhammad and God, or, in other words, insist that they have different natures. But those produced during his time in Medina indicate a '*narrowing of the functional gap between God and Muhammad*' (Marshall's italics).[10] After the Battle of Badr, the Qur'ān

---

[10] David Marshall, *God, Muhammad and the Unbelievers*: 170.

increasingly links the actions and status of God with the actions and status of Muhammad.

In Mecca, Muhammad was repeatedly reminded that he was only to warn unbelievers and that the impending consequences of their disobedience were entirely in the hands of God. In other words, he was reminded that judgement belongs only to God. In Medina, however, there developed what Marshall describes as 'the Godward movement of Muhammad and the umma'. They became active agents in punishing unbelievers on behalf of God. Muhammad, to use the words of the Egyptian Muslim writer Sherif Faruq, 'is joined to Allah as the source of absolute command'.[11] That is why the Sunna is coupled with the Qur'ān to complete revelation and provide the basis of law in Islam. Christians are apprehensive about this seeming joining of a fallible human being to God Almighty.

The Islamic doctrine of *isma*, or the infallibility of prophets in general and Muhammad in particular, is a later development. In the Qur'ān, only Jesus and Mary are described as sinless; Muhammad is said to be a mere mortal and a sinner (59:6–7; 47:19). But in the Sunna and within the framework of the Shari'ah (not to talk of popular Muslim devotion, where in some cases Muhammad is even elevated above God!) it is very difficult, if not impossible, to differentiate Muhammad's actions and status from those of God and vice versa. The theological difficulty Christians have with the Sunna is the real risk of attributing fallible human actions, mistakes and even wickedness to God. To express the Christian concern in another way, while Islam may be uncompromising in its insistence that God and Muhammad are fundamentally different, in practice their functions and duties are too closely intertwined for comfort.

Christians are particularly anxious about giving exclusively divine prerogatives such as judgement and punishment for unbelief to a mortal. According to Christian teaching, God is the only righteous judge and all others, including prophets, will stand before his judgement throne. Christians are repeatedly warned against passing judgement on others (Matt 7:1–2). The Bible clearly states that 'there is one lawgiver and judge, he who is able to save and to destroy. But who are you that you judge your neighbour?' (Jas 4:12). In other words, as far as Christian teaching is concerned, God is not only the lawgiver, but also the only

---

[11] Quoted in D. Marshall, *God, Muhammad and the Unbelievers*: 174.

judge. The power to save or destroy (i.e. accuse, convict, sentence and execute the sentence) lies solely with God. Moreover, Christians argue that a God who is unable to act to accomplish his own wishes and carry out his own decrees must also be unable to will and to decree.

Another area of Christian concern relates to the Muslim understanding of the Shari'ah as the solution to the human condition. As stated above, Islamic teaching depicts God as a sovereign ruler and people as his servants or slaves. In this master–servant relationship, the master wills, decrees and commands and the servant simply submits and obeys. Lack of knowledge or ignorance of the master's wishes is therefore the most fundamental problem of humanity. The Shari'ah as divine law meets this need and provides a solution to the problem. It is only by following the Shari'ah that Muslims can please God and gain success in this world and the next. Muslims therefore contend that

> Islam holds man to be not in need of any salvation. Instead of assuming him to be religiously and ethically fallen, Islamic *da'wah* acclaims him as the *khalifah* of Allah, perfect in form, and endowed with all that is necessary to fulfil the divine will indeed, even loaded with the grace of revelation! 'Salvation' is hence not in the vocabulary of Islam. *Falah*, or the positive achievement in space and time of the divine will, is the Islamic counterpart of Christian 'deliverance' and 'redemption'.[12]

Before expressing the Christian concerns on the Islamic position set out here, let us first lay out the Christian teaching on this issue. First of all, while acknowledging God as king, ruler and master, Christian teaching also depicts him as a father and humanity as his children, created in his image. As a father, God loves humanity deeply and longs for their well-being at all times and at any cost. Human beings are required to return this divine love in obedience and submission. While in Islam obedience seems to be motivated by fear or by hope of reward, in Christianity it should spring from inner delight, desire and love of God. Unfortunately, humanity often chooses the path of disobedience and rebellion. The Christian doctrines of the fall of man and original sin are attempts to acknowledge and explain this human tendency to waywardness and rebellion. The concept of original sin in Christianity is not to be taken as suggesting that every human being is a condemned sinner before birth. Arne Rudvin observes that Christians

> recognise that empirical and practical man is in an awful mess, and that all men are in the same mess, and have been throughout history, but we deny – or we insist, we cry out – that this is not what man was created to be. Man is not a sinner of necessity, but by his own will.[13]

As far as Christianity is concerned, the fundamental problem of humanity is not ignorance but disobedience, epitomised in Adam and Eve's eating of the fruit of the forbidden tree (Gen 3:1–6). The mess in which humanity has found itself in the past and present is the consequence of the innate tendency to wilful disobedience or rebellion. Humanity's basic need is thus salvation and, therefore, a saviour. In response to this need, Christians believe that God sent his own Son in the person of Jesus Christ to pay the ultimate penalty of sin, that is, death. Salvation is thus a free gift from God, obtained through faith in Jesus Christ.

Charles Adam has analysed the Islamic and Christian perspectives well. He summarises the Islamic perspective as ignorance > guidance > success, and the Christian perspective as sin > redemption > salvation.[14]

Just as Muslims find it hard to accept the Christian doctrine of original sin, so Christians find the Islamic diagnosis of the human condition difficult to comprehend. Muslim teaching fails to take the recalcitrant and rebellious nature of humanity seriously. People dispute and reject what may appear to be obvious truth, even divine truth. The fact that Muhammad did not just preach but *warned*, and even had to resort to the use of force, shows that people are recalcitrant. By insisting that political power or the exercise of authority is essential for actualising the divine will (as contained in the Shari'ah), Muslims are admitting this reality even if Islamic teaching refuses to acknowledge it. If people are 'perfect in form, and endowed with all that is necessary to fulfil the divine will', why do Islamic countries need religious police to enforce times of prayers, fasting, the dress code and other duties?

---

[13] Arne Rudvin, 'Comments' in *Christian Mission and Islamic Da'wah*: 47.
[14] See Charles Adam, 'Islam and Christianity: The opposition of similarities', in R. Savory and D. Aguis (eds.), *Logos Islamikos: Studia Islamica in Honorem Georgii Michaelis Wickens* (Toronto: Pontifical Institute of Medieval Studies, 1984).

Closely related to each religion's diagnosis of the human condition is its prescription for dealing with it. Like Muslims, Christians believe in divine laws or commandments and therefore they take the Ten Commandments seriously (Exod 20:1–17). Jesus underscored the importance of divine law by telling his audience, 'think not that I have come to abolish the law and the prophets; I have come not to abolish them but to fulfil them' (Matt 5:17). However, in fulfilling the law Jesus countered all legalism with radical love, even to his enemies:

> You have heard that it was said, 'You shall love your neighbour and hate your enemy.' But I say to you, Love your enemies and pray for those who persecute you (Matt 5:43–44).

Again, when he was asked about the greatest and most important of the commandments or laws of God, Jesus' reply was

> 'You shall love the Lord your God with all your heart, and with all your soul, and with all your mind.' This is the great and first commandment. And a second is like it: 'You shall love your neighbour as yourself' (Matt 22:37–39).

The key concern of Jesus' mission was 'to overcome legalism by fulfilment of the Will of God in love, in view of the coming Kingdom'.[15] Jesus not only taught this but also demonstrated it in his actions, deliberately breaking the letter of the law in order to uphold its spirit. This can be seen in his saving of a woman caught in adultery from being stoned to death and in the many instances in which he healed and performed various miracles on the Sabbath. All these angered those who regarded themselves as custodians of God's law.

While Muslims can justify the application of the Shari'ah by referring to Muhammad's example, it would be a betrayal of the mission of Jesus Christ if Christians were to support the Shari'ah and all its legalism. This is so because 'the law was given through Moses; [while] grace and truth came through Jesus Christ' (John 1:17). For Christians, the Muslim emphasis on law is, in many ways, an inversion of the progression from the Old Testament to the New.

---

[15] Hans Küng, 'Christianity and world religions: The dialogue with Islam as one model', in *The Muslim World*, Vol. 77, No. 2 (Apr. 1987): 89.

Islamic and Christian teaching on the status and place of law can be summarised as follows: In Islam, *falah* (success) is obtained by faith through works or observance of the law; in Christianity, salvation is by grace through faith in Jesus Christ. In line with the teaching of Jesus, Paul reminded the Ephesian Christians that 'by grace you have been saved through faith; and this is not your own doing, it is the gift of God' (Eph 2:8). Therefore 'a man is not justified by works of the law but through faith in Jesus Christ ... because by works of the law shall no one be justified' (Gal 2:16).

This teaching on grace does not mean that Christians have licence to violate divine injunctions. The Apostle Paul anticipated this misconception, for after reminding Christians that they are no longer under the bondage of the law, he quickly adds, 'What then? Shall we sin because we are not under law but under grace? By no means!' (Rom 6:15).

Muslims have often accused Christians of abdicating responsibility and only being interested in otherworldly matters. This accusation is not without foundation, for certain traditions of Christian teaching lend themselves to this tendency. However, mainstream Christian teaching as a whole and the example of Jesus in particular indicate that Christians ought to pray and actively seek the fulfilment of God's will in their private and public lives. They share with Muslims a belief in the importance of submission to the will of God in all aspects of human existence. In fact, Jesus made this point very forcefully when he said, 'Not every one who says to me, "Lord, Lord", shall enter the kingdom of heaven, but he who does the will of my Father who is in heaven' (Matt 7:21). The Lord's Prayer begins, 'Our Father who art in heaven, Hallowed be thy name. Thy kingdom come. Thy Will be done, on earth as it is in heaven' (Matt 5:9–10). This prayer, as John Onaiyekan has rightly pointed out,

> is not just a vague wish, or a pious aspiration for divine intervention in some remote future. Rather, it is a programme of action to which we are personally and resolutely committed. We too have a duty 'to command what is right and forbid what is evil'.[16]

We shall indicate the way Christians seek to accomplish this task shortly. It is, however, important to point out that the difference between Islamic and Christian teaching in this regard does not concern whether

---

[16] John Onaiyekan, 'The Shari'a in Nigeria: A Christian view', in *Encounters*, No. 133 (Mar. 1987): 7.

God's will *can* be actualised in the world but *how* this should be done. For Muslims, it must be enforced by the umma.

The main Christian reservation about the role of the umma as enforcers of God's will on earth has to do with the way God is depicted as standing in need of help from believers (3:52; 47:7; 57:25; 59:8; 9:40 etc.). The concept of believers (Muslims) being God's helpers has very serious implications, especially as it affects the relationship between Muslims and non-Muslims. As noted earlier, the God of the Qur'an is harsh and severe with unbelievers. In Mecca, the punishment of unbelievers was understood to be the task of God alone – a divine prerogative. In Medina, especially after the Battle of Badr, God delegates this task to Muhammad and the umma.

To put the Christian concerns expressed here into perspective, the Islamic and Christian positions can be summarised as follows. In Islam, God as creator revealed his will in the Qur'an and Sunna, which are manuals and guide for humanity. The umma's duty is to see to the enforcement of God's will in the world through the exercise of authority. The Christian teaching is that God the creator revealed himself in the person of Jesus to save humanity. The Holy Spirit enforces God's will by prompting, convicting and guiding, and the church witnesses by influencing the world as salt and light. So for Muslims to seek to enforce God's will in the form of the Shari'ah in its entirety in a shared environment with Christians is like Christians seeking to impose their belief in the Trinity upon Muslims.

A final theological concern an evangelical Christian would have with the Shari'ah has to do with the key injunction which grants Christians in an Islamic state the right to confess but not to proclaim their faith. They may not share their faith with Muslims or even express it openly and loudly for Muslims to hear. Proclamation is, however, an essential part of Christian confession of faith, just as it is in Islam. Jesus did not only call on people to believe in him, but also sent them out to bear witness to what they believed. Proclamation or witness is therefore as integral a part of Christianity as it is of Islam. It is against this background that Christians find the restriction and criminalisation of their witness very painful and unacceptable. For Christians, supporting the Shari'ah, which explicitly denies them the right to freely proclaim their faith and many other issues central to their belief, amounts to signing their confessional death warrant.

12

Key Theological and Missiological Questions

Any meeting with Muslims and engagement with Islam is bound to raise fundamental questions for Christians. Indeed, the claims of Islam discussed in the preceding chapters, especially in relation to Christianity, raise fundamental theological and missiological questions for Christian thought and witness in an Islamic context. This chapter will discuss four of these questions.

Do Muslims and Christians worship the same God?

One of the most frequently asked questions is whether Muslims and Christians worship the same God. From my own experience, when this question is put to ordinary believers on both sides, the overwhelming majority will answer in the affirmative. But when the same question is put to Christian pastors or Muslim religious figures, the majority are likely to answer in the negative. What I have chosen to do here is state the grounds upon which one could answer this question.

The first point that needs to be made is that if Christians and Muslims agree that there is only one God, the creator of the universe and of humanity, and both claim they are worshipping this God, then clearly they are both worshipping the same God. Secondly, given the Qur'ānic claim that Muhammad's prophetic mission is in line with the missions of such biblical figures as Abraham, Moses and Jesus, it is difficult to say that the God of Islam is not the same as the God of Christianity. Nothing in the Qur'ān suggests that Muhammad ever thought of Jews and Christians as worshipping a different God. On the contrary, Muslims are admonished in the Qur'ān to say:

> We believe in Allah and that which is revealed unto us and that which was revealed unto Abraham, and Ishmael, and Isaac, and Jacob, and the tribes, and that which Moses and Jesus received, and that which the Prophets received from their Lord. We make no distinction between any of them, and unto Him we have surrendered (2:136).

Thirdly, linguistically, *Allah* is simply the Arabic name for the High God or Supreme Being. In other words, the term 'Allah' is to Arabic speakers as 'God' is to English speakers, *Onyame* to Twi speakers in Ghana, *Oludumare* to the Yoruba in Nigeria, and *Ukulunkulu* to Zulus in South Africa. Arab Christians refer to God as Allah, and would never think of using a different term. Similarly Hausa Christians in West Africa use the term Allah for God and the Hausa Bible uses the term Allah throughout for God. So there is no linguistic justification for suggesting Allah is different from the Christian God. Writing as a Christian, David Shenk has no doubt that 'Christians and Muslims worship the same God'. He states that 'the name Allah is affirmed by Christians as one of the names of God. The Prophet Abraham knew God as El or Elohim, which is a Hebrew form of the Arabic Allah.'[1] Writing as a Muslim, Badru Kateregga also says:

> When Christians and Muslims talk about God, they are talking about the same God, although their witnessing concerning God may be rather different. When they speak of God, Allah, Yahweh or Elohim, they mean the God Who is the Only One, the Creator, the Loving, the Just, the Holy, the Merciful, the Living and Eternal, the Wise and Knowing. Nevertheless, the Christian witness emphasizes the self disclosure of God (hence the 'Trinity'), while in Islam it is the will and guidance of God which is revealed.[2]

Yet Kateregga's words also reveal that even where they are prepared to recognise the common ground between Muslim and Christian teaching

---

[1] Badru D. Kateregga and David W. Shenk, *Islam and Christianity.* 8.
[2] Kateregga and Shenk, *Islam and Christianity.* 88.

about God, Muslims are hesitant to state without qualification that the Christian God is the same as the Islamic God.

As if to underline the difference, all English translations of the Qur'ān retain the word 'Allah' rather than using the English equivalent, 'God'. Muslim governments in Malaysia and elsewhere have banned Christians from using the term 'Allah' in their translations of the Bible. In 1994, when there was fighting between the largely Muslim Dagomba and the largely Christian Konkomba in Northern Ghana, the Christian and Muslim leaders met and issued a statement calling upon the warring factions 'in the name of God and in the name of Allah' to stop fighting. This statement suggests that 'God' and 'Allah' are different entities. Thus although Colin Chapman asserts that 'it may be hard to find any *theological* [his emphasis] reason for trying to distinguish between the words "Allah" and "God" in Christianity',[3] the major differences between the Muslim and Christian witness to God do, in fact, lie in the area of doctrine and theology, and specifically relate to the doctrines of Tawhid and the Trinity.

Muslims are anxious to prevent any confusion between 'Allah, the one true God'[4] and the Christian God (the 'Trinity'):

> Because God is one and one only, to associate any being with God is a sinful and an infidel act. Islam makes it clear that God has no son, no father, no brother, no wife, no sister and no daughters ... In His unity, God is not like any other person or thing that can come to anyone's mind. His qualities and nature are conspicuously unique. He has no associates.[5]

To put it mildly, Muslims are very suspicious of and uncomfortable with the Christian idea of the Trinity and with Jesus being the Son of God. Islam regards any such association of another being with God as *shirk*, the unforgivable sin. They dismiss Christian explanations that belief in One Lord and One God and the Sonship of Jesus must be understood in spiritual, not physical, terms and insist that the doctrine of the Trinity is anthropomorphic.

---

[3] Colin Chapman, *Cross and Crescent: Responding to the Challenge of Islam* (Leicester: Inter-Varsity Press, 1995): 230.
[4] Kateregga and Shenk, *Islam and Christianity*: 1–2.
[5] Ibid.: 2.

It could, however, be argued that the argument here is not so much about the doctrines of Tawhid and the Trinity, and thus about the nature of God himself, as it is about the nature of God's relationship with humanity. The doctrine of Tawhid is the Islamic attempt to emphasis the absolute unity and uniqueness of God in order to stress that he is completely separate from his creation. The doctrine of the Trinity, on the other hand, is the Christian attempt to make sense of what are seen as three major divine movements and engagements with the created order in general and with humanity in particular. 'Father' refers to God as the creator, originator, head and owner of the universe. 'Son' refers to God's unfailing love and redemption of the world, and 'Holy Spirit' refers to God's continued presence, involvement and transforming power in the world. The doctrine of the Trinity seeks to underline the point that God is not only a God of communion, a God of dialogue and a God of relationship, but also a God *in* communion, *in* dialogue and *in* relationship. Christians and Muslims agree that God is the creator, master and sovereign lord over the whole of creation. The issue at stake, however, is how the Creator relates to his creation.

Both Muslims and Christians believe in revelation, that is, that God takes the initiative to reach out to humanity. Both agree that without revelation there could be no relationship between human beings and God. But that is as far as the agreement goes! Disagreement arises as soon we look at the nature of the revelation. According to Islam, God reveals his will, and the record of this revelation is 'in perfection in the Qur'ān'.[6] Christianity, on the other hand, teaches that God reveals not only his will but also himself in the person of Jesus of Nazareth. The question that then arises is, to what extent does the will of God contained in the Qur'ān match the life and ministry of Jesus as contained in the Gospels? If it can be argued that there is no match, is this sufficient grounds for saying the God whose will is contained in the Qur'ān cannot be the same God who revealed himself in Jesus Christ in the Gospels?

While the Christian witness accepts the transcendence of God as creator, master and ruler, it goes on to argue for what Kenneth Cragg refers to as 'divine responsibility' or 'involvement' with his creation and particularly with humanity.[7] Cragg draws an analogy with the example

[6] Isma'il al-Faruqi, in *Christian Mission and Islamic Da'wah*: 48.
[7] See a fascinating discussion between Kenneth Cragg and Isma'il al-Faruqi on the subject in *Christian Mission and Islamic Da'wah*: 47–51.

of kingship in Shakespeare's *Henry V*, 'when the king lays the crown aside and shows a simple concern to get alongside the common soldier in a dire situation', and asks rhetorically: 'Is this less kingly than sitting in the palace on a throne?' Al-Faruqi, responding to Cragg, states, 'If you are saying that the king next started polishing the soldier's shoes and carrying his ordinance box, then this is not kingly.'[8] The problem is that this is precisely the Christian witness about Jesus, the Son of God, who,

> being in very nature God, did not consider equality with God something to be grasped, but made himself nothing, taking the very nature of a servant, being made in human likeness. And being found in appearance as a man, he humbled himself and became obedient to death – even death on the cross (Phil 2:6–8).

In John 13:5–14, Jesus even went a step further than polishing shoes and carrying an ordinance box – he washed the feet of his disciples! The Muslim witness, which seeks to emphasise and jealously guard the complete transcendence and sovereignty of God, regards this as going too far! The relationship between God and humanity in Islam is that of master–servant or sovereign–subject, with clear and strictly defined roles. Polishing shoes, carrying ordinance boxes and washing feet are the duties of servants, not kings, and anyone who does these duties cannot be a king. Muslims therefore regard the Christian teaching on divine involvement as compromising the transcendence and sovereignty of God.

The Muslim God will not, cannot, and need not do the things the Christian God does. 'Allah is not begotten and does not beget' is the central teaching of the Qur'ān; 'Jesus is the Son of God' is the central teaching of Christianity. So can Allah be the Father of Jesus Christ?[9] If the Muslim answer is *no*, is it fair and right for Christians to insist that Jesus is the Son of the Muslim God? And if Allah is not the Father of Jesus, can it be said that Muslims and Christians worship the same God?

---

[8] Isma'il al-Faruqi, *Christian Witness and Islamic Da'wah*. 51.

[9] Note that the issue here has nothing do with any understanding or lack of understanding of the central teachings of Christianity. As shown in chapter ten, Muslims believe that the Islamic teaching on Jesus was revealed to them by God.

But there is another important precedent in the Bible that we cannot afford to ignore when answering the question as to whether the Muslim God is the same as the Christian God. It has to do with Paul and the altar to the Unknown God erected by the people of Athens (Acts 17:22–23). Colin Chapman notes that Paul did not hesitate to use the word *theos* (God) for both the Unknown God of the Athenians and the God who raised Jesus from the dead. Chapman concludes that Paul 'believed that there is enough in common between the concept of God in the mind of these pagan Greeks and his concept of God for him to use the same word'.[10] This may well be the case. But it must not be forgotten that Paul's basic motivation in this context was purely missionary and evangelistic. He was using the Unknown God of the Athenians as a stepping stone to present them with God the creator of the universe and the Father of Jesus Christ. In the same way, Allah or the Muslim God is a crucial stepping stone for sharing the Christian witness to God with Muslims.

Is Muhammad a Prophet of God?

In interfaith dialogue Muslims often emphasise that Islam accords Jesus a very special place. He is revered as a prophet of God, who was singularly endowed with many miracles, and they look forward to his second coming. They thus wonder why Christians cannot reciprocate this gesture by accepting Muhammad as prophet. This is a very sensitive question for Muslims, especially in the light of past Western Christian vilification and demonisation of Muhammad. In fact a few Muslims have stated categorically that until Christians reciprocate on the status of Muhammad and other truth claims in Islam, there can be no genuine dialogue.

In their attempts to respond, some Christian scholars have acceded that Muhammad can be regarded by Christians as a prophet in one sense or another, while others go so far as to say that there is no reason why Christians cannot accept Muhammad as a prophet as Muslims see him. Many Christians, without answering this question directly, simply use the title 'the Prophet' to refer to Muhammad.

---

[10] Colin Chapman, *Cross and Crescent*: 229.

If the question is taken at face value, Muslims have a good case in asking Christians to recognise Muhammad as a prophet of God, if only for the sake of good Christian–Muslim relations. But the question is not as simple and straightforward as it appears. For instance, Muslims do not profess that Muhammad is a prophet among other prophets. Rather, they profess that he is the last prophet of God, the Seal of the Prophets, who brought the final revelation in the form of the Qur'an, ushering in the last and perfect religion in the form of Islam. Therefore, to accept Muhammad as a prophet in line with Old Testament prophets or in any limited sense, as some like Kenneth Cragg have suggested,[11] amounts to a reduction of the Muslim belief. Many Muslims would rightly reject this. Here is one response to Kenneth Cragg's 'reductionism' in respect of the role and status of Muhammad:

> From the Muslim point of view Cragg's generous suggestion that Christians should regard Muhammad as 'the Prophet of the Qur'an' is not as generous as he thinks. For, Muslims do not recognize Muhammad only as 'the Prophet of the Qur'an' but as *Rasul Allah*, the Messenger of God. According to this belief, Muhammad is not just a Prophet for the Arabs but a Prophet with a universal Message for all human beings. Hence, Cragg's recognition of Muhammad as 'the Prophet of the Qur'an' is for Muslims nothing less than a betrayal of their faith.[12]

Aydin goes on to state that 'it is very difficult for a sensible Christian not to use the title "Prophet" for Muhammad' and that 'Christians who refuse to use the title "Prophet" for Muhammad offend Muslims and make it difficult to establish better relations with them'.[13]

Some Christian scholars therefore insist that Muhammad is a prophet of God and that Christians must acknowledge him as Muslims do.

---

[11] See the publication put out by the Conference of European Churches, *Witness to God in Secular Europe* (Geneva, 1984): 56, which calls on Christians to acknowledge Muhammad as a prophet in line with Old Testament prophets. See also Kenneth Cragg, *Muhammad and the Christian: A question of response* (London: Longman & Todd, 1984) in which Cragg suggests that Muhammad can be seen as 'the Prophet of the Qur'an'.

[12] Mahmut Aydin, 'Contemporary Christian evaluations of the prophethood of Muhammad', *Encounters: Journal of Inter-Cultural Perspectives,* Vol. 6, No. 1 (Mar. 2000): 42. See also Jabal Buaben, *Image of the Prophet Muhammad in the West: A study of Muir, Margoliouth and Watt* (Leicester: The Islamic Foundation, 1996).

[13] Mahmut Aydin, 'Contemporary Christian': 54.

Norman Daniel, for instance, suggests that 'it is essential for Christians to see Muhammad as a holy figure; to see him, that is, as Muslims see him ... if they do not do so, they must cut themselves off from Muslims'.[14] The difficulty with this position is that it is naïve, if not hypocritical, to think one can see Muhammad 'as Muslims see him' and yet remain non-Muslim. If we are really honest with ourselves and do justice to the Muslim faith, to see Muhammad as Muslims see him requires responding favourably to his message and so, inevitably, converting to Islam. To put it in perspective, for Muslims to demand that Christians acknowledge Muhammad as a prophet is like Christians demanding that Muslims accept Jesus as the Son of God and God Incarnate. These demands are asking partners in dialogue to commit confessional suicide! This, for many believers, is surely too great a price to pay for interfaith dialogue.

Two main responses can be made to the argument that Muslims accord a lot of respect to Jesus and accept him as a prophet. First, Muslim belief in Jesus as a prophet is not an ecumenical gesture intended to enhance relations between Muslims and Christians. It is an integral part of Islamic teaching. In this teaching, the role and status accorded to Jesus in relation to Muhammad are like those accorded to John the Baptist in relation to Jesus in the New Testament. In other words, the Muslim recognition of Jesus as a prophet, to quote the French Islamicist, Jacques Jomier, 'does not cost them anything'.[15] Secondly, many Christians view the Muslim belief in Jesus as a prophet as a rejection of their faith, for to Christians Jesus is far more than a prophet. He is the final and definitive revelation not *from* God but *of* God. Jesus is the Son of God, Emmanuel, God with us, the Saviour and Lord of humanity.

The truth of the matter is that the Muslim belief in Muhammad as a Prophet and the Christian belief in Jesus as the Son of God are confessional rather than factual statements. It behoves *believers*, not 'sensible' persons, to affirm them. In my view non-Muslims, especially Christians, can only refer to and respect Muhammad as the 'Prophet of Islam'.

---

[14] Norman Daniel, *Islam and the West: The Making of an Image* (Oxford: Oneworld, 1993): 336.
[15] Jacques Jomier, *How to Understand Islam*, trans. J. Bowden (London: SCM Press, 1989): 140.

Will Muslims (and People of Other Faiths) Be Saved?

Before addressing the question of whether non-Christians can be saved, we need to address a related question: Is Jesus the only way of salvation? The witness of the New Testament leaves the centrality of Jesus in God's scheme of things in no doubt. Creation is not only through him but for him; everything is fulfilled in him, everything necessary for salvation has been accomplished in him, and all of history will be drawn together in him. The New Testament is also clear that 'God so loved the world that he gave his one and only Son, that whoever believes in him shall not perish but have eternal life' (John 3:16). The *world* and *whoever* here are significant indicators of the all-inclusive nature of Jesus' mission. He is sent for the whole world, not only for Jews.

The New Testament also makes it abundantly clear that there is no other way or shortcut to reconciling humanity to God besides the cross. All the Gospels demonstrate that the only way for Jesus in his mission was the cross. As Ida Glaser puts it:

> From the time of the temptation in the wilderness he was again and again tempted to avoid it. Even his closest friends wanted to spare him, but he saw in this the same, satanic temptation. The climax is seen in Gethsemane, where he prays in agony, 'Father, if you are willing, take this cup from me' (Luke 22:42). Three times the only Son prays to the Father. Surely here, if any other way were possible, God would have provided it. Surely he would have heeded the Son's tears and blood. But he who spared Abraham the sacrifice of his son would not spare Jesus the cross. There was no other way.[16]

Glaser rightly concludes that if Jesus is the Saviour for everyone, then 'there need be no other. If the cross was necessary to deal with the sins of the world, there can be no other'.[17] The witness of the New Testament is, therefore, summed up in Jesus' declaration, 'I am the way and the truth and the life. No one comes to the Father except through

---

[16] Ida Glaser, *The Bible and Other Faiths: What does the Lord Require of Us?* (Leicester: Inter-Varsity Press, 2005): 188.
[17] Ibid.: 191.

me' (John 14:6). Any faithful reading of the New Testament cannot run away from this central witness.

But does the New Testament witness that Jesus is the Saviour for everyone and that the cross is the only way of salvation mean that Muslims and all people of other faiths, are not (and cannot be) saved? Does it mean that they are doomed to perdition?

The modern debate about the spiritual vitality and authenticity or otherwise of non-Christian religions and the place of adherents of these religions in God's plan of salvation flows from theological questions first raised within the context of Christian world mission conferences, first in 1910 in Edinburgh, then in 1928 in Jerusalem, and then at the 1938 conference in Madras, India. The point that came to preoccupy the minds of proponents of interfaith dialogue in general and those engaged in Christian–Muslim dialogue in particular has to do with the question of 'salvation' for adherents of other religious traditions, or, in other words, with the ability or otherwise of other religious traditions to bring their members to salvation. Three dominant theological positions have emerged:

- *Exclusivism*, in line with traditional Christian teaching, maintains that Jesus Christ (and by implication Christianity) is the only true way of salvation. All who follow other faiths are eternally lost unless they convert to Christianity.
- *Inclusivism* views Jesus Christ and Christianity as representing the whole truth but goes on to admit that in a mysterious way this truth can be found in other religions, albeit without the knowledge of the adherents of these traditions. Karl Rahner refers to this as 'anonymous Christianity' and Raimon Panikkar calls it the 'unknown Christ'. The inclusivist view holds that followers of different religious traditions may be saved through this unknown (and therefore unacknowledged) truth in their religious traditions, rather than through the various traditions the members actually confess. In this case, followers of Islam, for instance, can be saved not in their capacities as Muslims but as 'anonymous Christians'.
- *Pluralism*, the third and dominant theological view, takes exception to the view that any one particular religion can claim to be the only valid means of salvation. According to this view, all religions are revelations from God, given at particular times in history within particular cultural contexts. There are therefore many true religions

through which salvation can be obtained. Paul Knitter speaks for all pluralists when he makes the following submission to Christians:

> Only if Christians are truly open to the possibility (which, I will argue below, is for Christians a probability bordering on a necessity) that there *are* many true, saving religions and that Christianity is one among the ways in which God has touched and transformed our world, only then can authentic dialogue take place.[18]

These positions cannot be discussed in detail in this book, but I do wish to raise some questions relating to the pluralist point of view, which, in the eyes of many, has become the theology of dialogue.

Firstly, the pluralist's main concern is that it is arrogant for Christians to claim that they alone have the truth and thus to exclude others from God's plan of salvation. This is a valid concern, but there is also a valid and opposing concern about the vigour and forthrightness with which pluralists have attempted to include others in God's plan of salvation. Is it any less arrogant to assume the right to include others in God's plan of salvation than it is to exclude them? Christians who hold either of these attitudes are arrogating to themselves the role of visa officials in the consulate of heaven here on earth. It is presumptuous, and indeed patronising, to think that people of other religious traditions need our verdict on the value of their traditions or their fate in the hereafter. Yet some individual members of other religious traditions have, in the name of 'reciprocity', called on Christians to acknowledge and accept the veracity of their truth claims before dialogue can take place. But any members of any religious tradition who think they need a Christian affirmation of their truth claims for whatever purpose are conceding to Christians the role of arbiters in religious matters! Indeed, many people of other faiths regard Christian pontification on the value of their religious traditions as at best presumptuous and at worst offensive.

Secondly, Christians have often been urged to abandon their truth claims regarding the uniqueness of Jesus Christ in order to create 'equality' with their partners in dialogue. As can be seen from the earlier quotation from Knitter, calls to revise or abandon truth claims

---

[18] Paul F. Knitter, *One Earth Many Religions: Multifaith Dialogue and Global Responsibility* (Maryknoll NY: Orbis Books, 1995): 30. See also John Hick, *God has Many Names* (Philadelphia: Westminster Press, 1980).

are directed mainly, if not exclusively, at Christians. It is assumed that people of other religions come to dialogue with no truth claims of their own and therefore feel 'unequal' before their Christian partners. But we all know that nothing could be farther from the truth! Muslims, for instance, come to dialogue with a lot of confidence in their own truth claims and make no apologies whatsoever for them. So if Christians have to abandon their truth claims for the sake of dialogue (as the pluralists require), while others unashamedly cling to their truth claims, wherein lies the 'equality'? And, of course, to ask people of other traditions to abandon their truth claims in the name of dialogue would be seen as yet another form of Christian imperialism.

Thirdly, the premise that truth claims constitute obstacles to Christian–Muslim dialogue has undermined, rather than enhanced, the course of dialogue. The impression has been created that dialogue with people of other religions means sacrificing the fundamental teachings of one's own faith. Consequently many Christians and followers of other religions now think that any attempt at interfaith dialogue amounts to compromising the basic tenets of their traditions. These impressions are narrow and misleading! It is not that questions of truth are irrelevant in the context of dialogue. Rather, it is one thing to raise questions and another to give answers with a certainty that implies that we are privy to the mind of God. The discussion on the salvific value of other religious traditions and the fate of their followers in God's plan of salvation, which has dominated the theological discussion in the name of dialogue, is a typical example of a question that needs to be approached with humility. I agree with Lesslie Newbigin when he cautions Christians that if we look to the Bible to answer questions such as whether Muslims will be saved or not 'we shall find ourselves faced either with silence or with contradiction'.[19] Acts 1:7 suggests that there are certain things which we are not meant to know and which should not be our concern now. Paul explicitly says that 'now we see in a mirror dimly, but then face to face. Now I know in part; then I shall understand fully, even as I have been fully understood' (1 Cor 13:12).

---

[19] Lesslie Newbigin, 'The Christian faith and the world religions', in John Hick and Brian Hebblethwaite (eds.), *Christianity and Other Religions: Selected Readings* (Oxford: Oneworld, 2001): 109.

The parable of the weeds in Matthew 13: 24–30, 36–43 has profound lessons for us with regard to the position Christians should take concerning the fate of people of other faiths:

- Contrary to the claim that all religions lead to God, there are counterfeit or false religions and, by implication, false or mistaken believers even within Christianity (Matt 7:21–23). These are the weeds in the parable.
- God knows this, but in his wisdom he has not only allowed the weeds to exist alongside the good seeds, but also blesses both equally with the same nutrients from the soil (Matt 5:43–48).
- Even if Christians consider themselves the wheat, they, like the servants in the parable, cannot identify the weeds. Christians cannot know for sure who are the children of the kingdom and who are not.
- Even if we think we know, it is not our duty to get rid of the weeds or send them packing to hell, so to speak, either physically or theologically. In other words, we have no right to judge. There is going to be a day of judgement when God will judge all things in his own time, in his own way.

In the New Testament Christians are commissioned to be witnesses (Acts 1:8). Throughout the book of Acts and the Epistles, the apostles reminded their audience that they were merely testifying to what they had witnessed of the life and works of Jesus as well as to his death, resurrection and ascension. A witness can only talk of things he or she has experienced. Teachers develop ideas and doctrines. Witnesses speak of the impact of these ideas and doctrines on their lives.

Let us use the metaphor of a courtroom to clarify how important it is that we have the right perspective on our role. In a courtroom, the principal characters are the judge, lawyers, witnesses and, of course, the accused and accuser. The lawyers are the ones who have to argue the case in order to seek conviction or acquittal; the witnesses are simply called upon to testify to what they have seen, heard or experienced. The judge has the task of passing judgment and sentencing the accused.

In biblical teaching, God (and Jesus at his second coming) is the one and only righteous judge with the power to pass judgement and impose sentences. The Holy Spirit plays the role of the lawyer, while Christians are simply called upon to be witnesses. We should guard against confusing our role with God's role. After all, the Bible warns us very clearly not to judge: 'Do not judge, or you too will be judged. For in the same way you judge others, you will be judged, and with the measure you use, it will be measured to you' (Matt 7:1–2). Paul warns us not to 'pronounce judgment before the time, before the Lord comes, who will bring to light the things now hidden in darkness and will disclose the purposes of the heart' (1 Cor 4:5). He is even more explicit when he asks, 'What business is it of mine to judge those outside the church? Are you not to judge those inside?' (1 Cor 5:12).

As far as I am concerned, the question should not be whether Muslims or people of other faiths can obtain salvation. The truth is that no one, including Christians, can obtain salvation by themselves. Similarly, no religion, including Christianity, can save. As Peter Cottrell observes, 'an individual may be saved in a religion or outside a religion, but cannot be saved by a religion'.[20] The issue therefore is *not* the ability of people of other faiths to attain salvation, or the validity of their religions in gaining them salvation. The issue here is God. Article Five of the Manila Manifesto of the Lausanne Movement states;

> The Scriptures declare that God himself is the chief evangelist. For the Spirit of God is the Spirit of truth, love, holiness and power, and evangelism is impossible without him. It is he who anoints the messenger, confirms the word, prepares the hearer, convicts the sinful, enlightens the blind, gives life to the dead, enables us to repent and believe, unites us to the body of Christ, assures us that we are God's children, leads us into Christ-like character and service, and sends us out in our turn to be Christ's witnesses.[21]

The issue is about God, the chief evangelist, having the power and freedom to directly reach out to all people wherever, whenever and however he chooses. And Christians know for sure that 'salvation belongs to God' (Rev 7:10); that salvation is a free gift from God (Matt 22:14, the parable of the wedding banquet; Matt 20:1–16, the parable of the workers); that God 'desires *all* people to be saved and to come to the knowledge of the truth' (1 Tim 2:4); and finally that 'what is impossible

[20] Peter Cottrell, *Mission and Meaninglessness* (London: SPCK, 1990): 80.
[21] Lausanne Movement, *Manila Manifesto*, <http://www.lausanne.org/Brix?pageID=12894>, accessed Dec. 2006

with men is possible with God' (Luke 18:27). These are what we know for sure for now, and these should form the core of Christian witness.

Should Christians Witness to Muslims?

Conflicts between religions have led many to argue that propagation of one's faith and converting others is not only incompatible with but detrimental to harmonious interfaith relations. Conversion is indeed a controversial issue, especially in places such as India and the former communist countries of Eastern Europe. It is punishable by death in mainline Islamic teaching. However, at the root of this controversy is the basic issue of the relationship between good relations between different faiths (or dialogue), and the propagation of one's faith. Some think that these are incompatible.[22]

At a Christian–Muslim consultation in 1976, a resolution was passed, under strong Muslim pressure, calling for the suspension of Christian missions in Muslim societies in order 'to cleanse the atmosphere of Christian–Muslim relations'.[23] Leaving aside the fact that those who made the call themselves knew that it was meaningless, in some parts of the world, and especially in Africa, evangelism or witness can be described as the heartbeat of the church! For many African Christians, calls for the suspension of witness sound like calls for ecclesiastical suicide, a price not worth paying for dialogue.

The truth is that Islam and Christianity are both missionary religions. Muslims are actively engaged in converting others right across the world, and they insist on their right to do so. Leading Muslim figures who head organisations engaged in the aggressive propagation of Islam in many parts of the world are also actively involved in interfaith dialogue. Their integrity is not generally called into question. But if there is no conflict of principle between the propagation of Islam and dialogue, why is there a problem with Christian mission and dialogue?

---

[22] See Byron L. Sherwin and Harold Kasimow (eds.), *John Paul II and Interreligious Dialogue* (Maryknoll NY: Orbis, 1999). One of the major criticisms levelled against Pope John Paul II was that while he actively encouraged evangelism, he also talked about dialogue with people of other religions.

[23] See the conference statement of a Christian–Muslim consultation organised by the World Council of Churches in Chambésy, Switzerland, in 1976 in *Christian Mission and Islamic Da'wah*: 100–101.

The real source of conflict, as far as I am concerned, lies in the inconsistency of those who encourage the propagation of their own faith but forbid the conversion of their own members. Denying people the right to change their religion is not just a violation of a universally accepted right of the individual but, even more importantly, a turning of religion into a prison whose followers become inmates condemned to a life sentence. No one wants to be in a prison, no matter how wonderful that prison might appear. Thus I believe that all missionary religions should endeavour to insist not only on the right to share their faith but on the right of people to change their religion. Even more importantly, any meaningful and genuine environment of religious pluralism must include (not exclude) freedom of speech, freedom of choice and freedom of association. Denial of any of these is a denial of the very fabric of pluralism.

Christians living as minorities in some parts of the Islamic world are often extremely nervous, even fearful, about bearing witness to Christ. Listening to and reading many of the works produced by Christians in India and parts of south-east Asia and the Middle East, one gets the feeling that some of them are driven by self-preservation. They speak and write against Christian witness because they do not want to disturb the status quo. I listened with amazement to a presentation by a theological college lecturer in which he questioned the need for Christian witness and the conversion of people of other religions. He insisted that 'in the Gospels we do not come across Jesus busy in changing the religion of the people'. He pointed out that, 'Mission as directed to the followers of other religions is a later interpretation, foreign to the Gospels.' He went on to call for 'a radical change in the Church's self-understanding and its mission with regard to other religions'.[24] One wonders how this attitude squares with the words of our Lord Jesus Christ in Luke 9:23:

> If any man would come after me, let him deny himself and take up his cross daily and follow me. For whoever would save his life will lose it; and whoever loses his life for my sake, he will save it. For what does it profit a man if he gains the whole world and loses or forfeits himself? For whoever is ashamed of

---

[24] Jacob Kavunkal, 'A theological response to globalization', paper presented at a Regional Consultation of Theological Institutions, Union Biblical Seminary, Pune, India (28–29 March 2001).

> me and of my words, of him will the Son of man be ashamed
> when he comes in his glory and the glory of the Father and of
> the holy angels.

Contrary to many people's assumptions, bearing witness to Christ does not mean attempting to change someone else's religion. It is merely presenting, by whatever means, one's experience of Christ and what the gospel is all about. What people of other religions do with the witness they receive from a Christian is in God's hands. They themselves must decide whether to change their religion and re-orientate their thinking if their current position no longer satisfies them or makes sense.

This is not to imply that Christian witness is easy or straightforward. Jesus knew that he was sending his disciples into difficult and hostile situations. He warned them, 'Behold, I send you out as sheep in the midst of wolves; so be wise as serpents and innocent as doves' (Matt 10:16). This was the rule the first Christians lived by and it should be the golden rule for Christian witness in any context.

The example of the apostles and of believers in the first three centuries as they endured severe persecution should serve both as a model and as inspiration for Christian witness in difficult situations. When Peter and John were threatened and ordered not to preach the gospel, the believers responded not by revising their truth claims or looking for an easy way out, but by praying for boldness (Acts 4). What the persecuted church needs is not so much new strategies and methods of evangelising as motivation and courage for witnessing and evangelism. The prayer for boldness in Acts 4:23–31 should be the model for Christian minorities in difficult situations.

For both Christians and Muslims, the right to witness to one's faith does not only involve freedom of speech and expression, but also freedom of religion. The two faiths enjoin both *confession* and *proclamation*. Jesus did not only call on people to believe in him; he also sent them out to bear witness to what they believed. Proclamation or witness is therefore as integral to Christianity as it is to Islam. To grant Christians the right to confess their faith, yet deny them the freedom to proclaim it, is like telling someone, 'You may breathe in but you may not breathe out'! Thus the restriction and criminalisation of Christian witness enshrined in the Shari'ah and enforced in many Muslim countries is very painful and unacceptable to Christians.

It is sometimes implied that because of the focus on proclamation, Christians can only see people of different religions as objects for conversion. But the Bible strongly condemns any treatment of people as objects. And if I may use myself as an example, given my own background, I see the members of my own family who are Muslim or who follow Traditional African Religion as my blood relations, and not as objects for evangelism! Above all, I see them as people created in the image of God deserving respect and love. It is against this background that I strongly believe in the right to persuade and be persuaded, while at the same time remaining a strong believer in dialogue.

My understanding is that propagation of one's faith is primarily concerned with bringing about a change in someone else's belief, and that dialogue is primarily concerned with interaction that changes our perceptions of and attitudes towards one another. Propagation and dialogue are not mutually exclusive!

As Christians we may think that our doctrines are correct. But for our understanding and response or witness to Islam and Muslims to be effective and glorifying to the Lord, we need to get the correct attitude that goes with the message. We must do more than merely preach about tolerance, love, humility, compassion, justice and equality. Our passion for witness and commitment to the gospel must be united with the fruit of the Holy Spirit as spelled out by Paul in Galatians 5:22. If it were, our witness to Muslims would be greatly enhanced. After all, the core message of the gospel is about relationships. And as Paul points out, we are entrusted with a gospel or ministry of reconciliation (2 Cor 5:18–19). The promotion of good relations should guide our intellectual and theological enquiries as well as our witness. But we must not sacrifice either our personal integrity or that of the gospel in the process. We need our roots in place if we are to be able to reach out to others.

Appendix

Key Qur'ānic Passages, Organised Thematically

God	2:255	sovereignty of God
	Sura 112	oneness of God (*Tawhid*)
	24:35–36	'Allah is the light' – a passage that has inspired mystics
	2:256	'there is no compulsion in religion'
	59:22–24	the most beautiful names of God
Creation	3:189–91; 13:2–4; 31:10–11; 32:4–9	
Heaven and Hell	2:24–25; 38:49–60; 44:47–57	
Prophets	2:124–34	
Laws	4:3	about marriage
	5:38	about theft
	2:275–79	about usury
	29:8	about obedience to parents
	2:219	about wine
	2:173	about pork
	2:83; 2:177	summary of the moral law
The Qur'ān	12:2; 46:12	revealed in the Arabic language
	33:40	Muhammad 'the seal of the prophets'
	5:15	Qur'ān reveals what Jews and Christians have hidden in their Scriptures
	2:106; 16:101; 22:52	abrogation (the belief that earlier recitations can be superseded by later ones)

(Continued)

The Bible	2:87; 3:3	*tawrat* or Torah recognised as revealed to Moses
	4:163	*zabur* or Psalms recognised as revealed to David
	5:46–48	*injil* or Gospel recognised as revealed to Jesus
	2:91; 3:1–4; 3:84	the message of previous scriptures confirmed by the *Qur'ān*
	5:48; 18:28	God has protected the Scriptures
	10:94–95	Muhammad told to consult the Scriptures already revealed if he is in doubt about what is revealed to him
Accusations against Jews and Christians	2:78	ignorant of their Scriptures
	2:146–59, 174; 5:15	conceal their Scriptures
	2:75	change their Scriptures
	2:79	sell false Scriptures for gain
	2:85	believe only parts of their Scripture
About Christians	2:62, 136–37; 5:69, 82; 22:40	sympathetic to Christians
	3:64–71; 29:46	appeals to Christians to accept Muhammad's message because it confirms the Gospel
	5:14, 51; 9:29–31; 57:27	critical of and even hostile to Christians
About Jesus	3:35–47; 19:16–35	the annunciation and birth of Jesus
	3:48–54; 5:110–17; 57:27; 61:6	the ministry of Jesus
	3:55; 4:155–59; 5:117; 19:33	the death of Jesus
	3:59; 4:171–72; 5:72–75, 116–17; 9:30–31	Jesus, God and the Trinity

Further Reading

What follows is not a bibliography of all works cited in this book, but rather a selected list of books that can be used to supplement the information given here. We have divided the books into three broad groups, although there will inevitably be some overlap in their contents.

General Works on Islam

Ayoub, M. Mahmoud, *Islam: Faith and History* (Oxford: Oneworld Publications, 2004).

— , *The Crisis of Muslim History: Religion and Politics in Early Islam* (Oxford: Oneworld Publications, 2003).

Cooper, Anne and Maxwell, Elsie A. (eds.), *Ishmael my Brother: A Christian Introduction to Islam* (London: Monarch Books, 2003).

Cragg, Kenneth, *The Call of the Minaret* (rev. ed., Oxford: Oneworld Publications, 2000).

Engineer, Asghar Ali, *Rethinking Issues in Islam* (Mumbai: Orient Longman, 1998).

Esack, Farid, *Qur'ān, Liberation and Pluralism: An Islamic Perspective of Interreligious Solidarity against Oppression* (Oxford: Oneworld Publications, 1997).

— , *The Qur'an: A User's Guide* (Oxford: Oneworld Publications, 2005).

Ishaq, I, *The Life of Muhammad: A Translation of Ibn Ishaq's Sirat Rasul Allah* (trans Alfred Guillaume) (Oxford: Oxford University Press, 1955).

Jomier, Jacques, *How to Understand Islam* (trans. J. Bowden) (London: SCM, 1989).

Lewis, Bernard, *Islam: From the Prophet Muhammad to the Capture of Constantinople*, vol. 1 *Politics and War* (New York: Harper & Row, 1974).

Marshall, David, *God, Muhammad and the Unbelievers: A Qur'anic Study* (London: Curzon Press, 1999).

Nasr S. H., *Traditional Islam in the Modern World* (London: Kegan Paul, 1990).

Nazir-Ali, Michael, *Islam: A Christian Perspective* (Exeter: Paternoster Press, 1983).

Rahman, Fazlur, *Islam* (Chicago: University of Chicago Press, 1979).

Rippin, Andrew, *Muslims: Their Religious Beliefs and Practices*. vol. 2: *The Contemporary Period* (New York: Routledge, 1993).

Safi, Omid (ed.), *Progressive Muslims on Justice, Gender, and Pluralism* (Oxford: Oneworld Publications, 2003).

Sarwar, Ghulam, *Islam: Beliefs and Teachings* (London: Muslim Educational Trust, 1992).

Schimmel, Annemarie, *And Muhammad Is His Messenger: The Veneration of the Prophet in Islamic Piety* (Chapel Hill, NC: University of North Carolina Press, 1985).

Watt, W. Montgomery, *Muhammad: Prophet and Statesman* (Oxford: Oxford University Press, 1964).

The World of Islam: Resources for Understanding Islam CD-ROM (Colorado Springs: Global Mapping International/Fuller Theological Seminary, 2000).

Islam in Africa

Alkali, N. et al. (eds.), *Islam in Africa: Proceedings of the Islam in Africa Conference* (Ibadan: Spectrum, 1993).

Azumah, John Alembillah, *The Legacy of Arab-Islam in Africa: A Quest for Inter-Religious Dialogue* (Oxford: Oneworld Publications, 2001).

Haafkens, J., *Islam and Christianity in Africa* (Nairobi: Desktop Publishers, 1992).

Hiskett, Mervyn, *The Course of Islam in Africa* (Edinburgh: Edinburgh University Press, 1994).

Mazrui, Ali, *The Africans: A Triple Heritage* (London: BBC, 1986).

Rosander, E. E., and Westerlund, D., (eds.), *African Islam and Islam in Africa: Encounters between Sufis and Islamists* (London: Hurst, 1997).

Sanneh, Lamin, *Piety and Power: Muslims and Christians in West Africa* (New York: Orbis, 1996).

— , *The Crown and the Turban: Muslims and West African Pluralism* (Boulder, Col: Westview, 1997).

Sulaiman, I., *Revolution in History: The Jihad of Usman Dan Fodio* (London: G. Mansell, 1986).

Trimingham, J. S., (ed.), *A History of Islam in West Africa* (Oxford: Oxford University Press, 1962).

— , *Islam in East Africa* (Oxford: Clarendon, 1964).

— , *Islam in Tropical Africa* (2nd ed. London: International African Institute, 1980).

Westerlund, D. and Rosander, E. E. (eds.), *African Islam and Islam in Africa: Encounters between Sufis and Islamists* (London: Hurst, 1997).

Islam and Christianity

Azumah, John, *Let Your Light Shine! Christian Witness in a Muslim Context* (Sydney: Horizons Publications, 2006).

Chapman, Colin, *Cross and Crescent: Responding to the Challenge of Islam* (Leicester: Inter-Varsity Press, 1995).

Cragg, K., *Jesus and the Muslim: An Exploration* (Oxford: Oneworld Publications, 1999).

Fernando, Ajith, *The Christian's Attitude Toward World Religions* (Mumbai: Gospel Literature Service, 1987).

Gaudeul, Jean-Marie, *Encounters and Clashes: Islam and Christianity in History, Vol. II* (Rome: Pontificio Istituto di Studi Arabi e d'Islamistica, 1984 & 2000).

— , *Called from Islam to Christ: Why Muslims become Christians* (Crowborough, UK: Monarch Books, 1999).

Glaser, Ida, The *Bible and Other Faiths: What does the Lord Require of Us?* (Leicester: Inter-Varsity Press, 2005).

Haddad, Y. Y. and Haddad, W., (eds.), *Christian–Muslim Encounters* (Miami: University of Florida Press, 1995).

Ipgrave, Michael (ed.), *The Road Ahead: A Christian–Muslim Dialogue* (London: Church House Publishing, 2002).

Kateregga, Badru and Shenk, David W., *Islam and Christianity: A Muslim and a Christian in Dialogue* (Nairobi: Uzima Press, 1980).

McAuliffe, Jane Dammen, *Qur'ānic Christians: An Analysis of Classical and Modern Exegesis* (Cambridge: Cambridge University Press, 1991).

Nazir-Ali, Michael, *Frontiers in Muslim-Christian Encounter* (Oxford: Regnum Books, 1987).

Peters, F. E., *Judaism, Christianity and Islam: The Classical Texts and Their Interpretation*, Vol. 2 (Princeton: Princeton University Press, 1990).

Robinson, Neal, *Christ in Islam and Christianity* (London: Macmillan, 1991).

Watt, William Montgomery, *Muslim-Christian Encounters: Perceptions and Misperceptions* (London: Routledge, 1991).

Ye'or, Bat and David Maisel, *The Dhimmi: Jews and Christians under Islam* (Madison, NJ: Fairleigh Dickinson University Press, 1985).

Zebiri, Kate, *Muslims and Christians Face to Face* (Oxford: Oneworld Publications, 1997).